ALSO BY GAVIN KENNEDY
Everything Is Negotiable!

WITH JOHN BENSON AND JOHN McMILLAN
Managing Negotiations

DOING BUSINESS ABROAD

GAVIN KENNEDY

SIMON AND SCHUSTER New York

215931

658.4
K 35

This is a revised edition of NEGOTIATE ANYWHERE! by Gavin
Kennedy, published in Great Britain by Business Books Ltd.
SIMON AND SCHUSTER and colophon are registered trademarks of
Simon & Schuster, Inc.
Designed by Irving Perkins Associates
Manufactured in the United States of America

1 2 3 4 5 6 7 8 9 10

Library of Congress Cataloging in Publication Data

Kennedy, Gavin.
    Doing business abroad.

    Rev. ed. of: Negotiate anywhere. c1985.
    Includes index.
    1. Negotiation in business.   2. Success in business.
3. Business enterprises—Foreign countries.   I. Kennedy,
Gavin.   Negotiate anywhere.   II. Title.
HD58.6.K45   1985   658.4   85-14416
ISBN: 0-671-55484-0

This publication is designed to provide accurate information, not legal
advice.

FOR KAREN

Contents

Preface

The most frequent question I get in my international negotiating seminars comes from negotiators who ask, "How do you rate negotiators from other countries?" This often leads to some of the most illuminating discussions we have at the Negotiators' Clinics, particularly when the participants are of mixed nationalities. Negotiators, from the most experienced through beginners, are always interested in each other's styles and whether this or that culture produces the "best" or most "natural" negotiators.

I have always insisted that there is no such thing as a born negotiator, and I am more than ready to assert that no one culture or nationality produces "better" negotiators than another. I firmly believe that negotiating is a skill that can be learned and that no matter what level of skill we have at any moment, we can all improve our performance by training and experience.

Just as firmly, I believe that people of different cultures have produced different styles of negotiating, whether in the pace at which they conduct their business or in the more common of the tactics they employ to secure their objectives. Add to this cultural background the unique economic and political features of a society and you have almost completely defined the content and method used in the negotiations in which its members are involved.

This book can be seen as a summation and extension of the

content of my seminars that deal with the importance of culture and background in the negotiating processes that the international business community finds necessary to conduct its wealth-creating foreign trade.

Doing Business Abroad makes no claim to being an exhaustive survey of every country and every culture in the world of business. I have selected some of the major trading areas in order to concentrate on important features that negotiators must consider if they want to do better.

I look at negotiating styles in both capitalist and Communist countries, in the Middle East, South America, Japan, and Europe. My central message is that you can negotiate abroad if you remember that culture does influence your partner's behavior; and that if you want to do better in your negotiations you had better become aware of the influence your partner's culture is exerting on him or her and, just as important, the extent to which you are influenced by your own culture.

I have met many hundreds of international negotiators over the past twelve years and many of them have influenced the contents of this book. To all of them I offer totally inadequate but nevertheless sincere thanks for all they have taught me.

My colleagues, John Benson and John McMillan, have continued to impress their individual and unique talents upon my thinking about negotiating, and in numerous instances in this book their influence has been instrumental in what I have said (though they are absolved from any responsibility for the way I have inadequately done justice to their clear thinking).

My family have been their usual helpful selves while I have been "fooling around" on my word processor.

The fact that the book has appeared at all is due to the support received from Frederic Hills at Simon and Schuster. That readers are the final arbiters of a book's merits has always guided my work, and I therefore extend to all my usual invitation to write (care of Simon and Schuster) and tell me your views. For information about my seminars, call Fred Slowick (Washington Speakers Bureau, Inc.) at (703) 684-0555.

Gavin Kennedy

Introduction

Negotiating is the name of the game

Negotiating is the name of the game. How to get better deals, how to improve your share of the cake—how to get a bigger cake for both of you!—that's what this book is about. And more!

Trade is an international activity. Of the over 160 countries in the world, all engage in trade, some more than others. This book is about negotiating in some of the major trading countries of the world.

We look at what is appropriate in some trading regions of the world—what to do and what not to do, the you-better-believe-its and the no-nos.

Business methods and ethics can vary across the globe. If you want to do business in foreign lands and with foreign traders you must get acquainted with their differing styles and approaches. They are not going to change to suit you and your way of life. You must change or get out of the international trading business.

This book is about doing business *anywhere* and not just in your own backyard. If you feel safer trading with Joe three blocks from your home, well and good. There is no compulsion for anybody to get into the international business scene; foreign trade is strictly for volunteers. But you owe it to yourself to look at the international picture before you dismiss it.

This is a practical, not a theoretical, survey of business negotiating. I have packed in much practical advice on the negotiating methods used by practical traders the world over. If the winners use these methods every day, you ought to learn about them and use them immediately.

Negotiating has a basic structure around the world, but the practical principles—how and when the shots are played—vary from business culture to business culture. What might be regarded as a necessary display of aggressive pricing in the United States could be taken as the ultimate in bad manners in Saudi Arabia; the Japanese may react to your personal manner and its associated mannerisms in an entirely different way from the Soviet trade official; the "leetle geeft for your wife" in the Philippines could get you into deep trouble in France; and what is good for business in the United States might be regarded as the height of folly in Germany.

Hence, the text is packed with examples of the different, and sometimes subtle, ways in which the negotiating shots are played across the globe. It does not matter for what stakes you are negotiating, big or small. The examples cover the entire spectrum from multimillion-dollar deals right down to the price of a taxi or a drink or a copy of your favorite newspaper at a newsstand in downtown Ogoland. Never neglect looking for lessons in every transaction you witness or participate in; they all have something to teach you about the business of trading.

Self-assessment tests

At the beginning of chapters 1 through 10 there are short (and painless!) self-assessment tests. Read the questions carefully and then mark the answer that you consider to be most appropriate, given the information available.

As you read the chapters you will see how I have approached the negotiating issues raised in the questions. My opinions on the answers (with purely nominal scores) are set out at the end of each chapter. The opinions I express are, of course, entirely my own and you might feel that you have good cause to differ with them. You may question my opinions and indeed, anybody else's, on negotiating!

I believe that the views I have expressed on negotiating situations represent the best practice for the majority of occasions I have chosen to illustrate in this way, but, as every negotiator knows, other people—sometimes the majority— see things differently from the way we do. That is why we need to negotiate! So I am not going to be upset if you decide to differ.

At our Negotiators' Clinics we have lively sessions when we discuss the answers that negotiators have chosen in contrast to mine. I am sometimes asked about the significance of the scores for the tests. The point is that the discussion of the answers is far more important than the size of your score, but if you get a high score in each test you can't be doing all that badly as a negotiator (though you might not realize that you can *always* do better). If you get a low score, you know you have room for improvement, which may not be so obvious to the high scorer. In a way, this gives you an edge, doesn't it?

DOING
BUSINESS
ABROAD

SELF-ASSESSMENT TEST 1

1 You are negotiating with a team of engineers at a large turbine factory in Wusan, China. There are eight people on their side of the table and three on yours. Two of your colleagues are from corporate headquarters in Milwaukee. How many foreigners are at the meeting?

a One
b Three
c Eight
d Ten

2 Just before you leave for a business trip to France, Congress passes (yet) another law with which you disagree completely. Over dinner in Paris you have an opportunity to give your views on the new law to your hosts. Do you:

a Give them the benefit of your detailed opinions on why the law ought not to have been passed?
b Merely report the bare facts and give a single-sentence argument for and against the measure?
c Tell them that you know little more about the new law than you read in the French papers that morning?
d Tell them you have no views on the law?
e Ask them how they see the new law?

3 You are waiting at Sharjah airport in the United Arab Emirates for a connection, and an Arab passes in front of you. A woman is following behind him, and she has her face covered with a leather mask. Do you:

a Comment on this to the stranger sitting next to you?
b Say nothing about it, not even in response to the stranger's comments?

CHAPTER 1

The Worst Thing You Can Do When Abroad—or, Foreigners, Damn Foreigners

Bad manners

What is the worst thing that you can do when negotiating abroad? Quite simply, it is to forget that it is you, not the other guy, who is the foreigner.

You are not in a foreign country, you are a foreigner in somebody else's homeland. The people there are not foreigners—they live there! *You* are the foreigner. You have the peculiar ways. You are the one out of step. You have the awkward mannerisms, and you are the object of curiosity. If you start off thinking otherwise, you will probably take a lot longer than you need, or expect, to get the business you feel you deserve.

To you, the United States may be God's little Eden, the finest land in the world and worthy of the utmost respect from those not privileged to live in it. And your beliefs are perfectly reasonable to you. But, please, spare those you travel the world to negotiate with your unsolicited and unrestrained eulogies about the land of your birth.

Not only is it bad manners to bore people with your fantasies, it can be downright insulting to be on the receiving end of someone's jingoistic ravings and the manners (or lack of them) that are based on unblemished superpatriotism, especially when your victims might have similar deeply felt emotions about their own country.

Pride in one's country is one thing, and perfectly harmless if handled discreetly, but ramming your pride down the other guy's throat is altogether unacceptable and, what is decisive, it is bad for business.

No matter where you come from on the planet, it is not the entire repository of the achievements of the human race. Other peoples, other places, other times all make their contribution to human progress and civilization.

How not to be a foreigner

I knew a negotiator who, having had a rewarding and steady career as a buyer in Chicago for a major international company, was sent to Italy to help integrate a newly acquired subsidiary into the European division. Although he had dealt with overseas agents for many years, his negotiating contacts with "foreigners" had been largely conducted by telephone and telex.

Henry had not worked abroad before but the head office had selected him for this temporary assignment because of his extensive experience as the company's buyer. Also, he was near retirement, and the posting would enable them to undertake some reorganization in the European division six months earlier than they had planned. Henry's successful completion of the assignment would not threaten anybody else's career progression (his absence, in fact, speeded up the promotion of several other executives), while failure was not expected, in view of his seniority and the relatively minor nature of the integration problems.

Within weeks, however, the specter of a disaster material-
ized. That something was going badly wrong with his assignment soon became apparent to Chicago. They did not at first
take the early reports too seriously, which was, in retrospect,
probably a mistake. Eventually, however, they decided that
they had to act, though they were not eager to rush in and
make changes without giving their much-esteemed executive
full benefit of their collective doubts.

They wanted an unbiased and independent report of what
was going on, or rather not going on, and I was asked to take
a look while I was passing through Italy on another assignment. On the basis of this report, if it was negative, they
would recall their executive and replace him with somebody
else.

The problem was essentially quite simple. Henry had gotten himself into a state by being extremely uptight about the
Italian style of doing business—and anything else, for that
matter—which is, broadly speaking, one of emotional volatil-
ity and intense haggling. He regarded them as "foreigners,
damn foreigners" and beyond redemption.

It started the moment he picked me up at Galileo Galilei
airport, Pisa, in his hired Mercedes. He moaned about Italian
road manners all the way to Luca. In his office he went on
and on about how long it took to get anything done. In his
splendid villa, high in the mountains overlooking the Tus-
cany coast, he bemoaned the work rate of the domestic staff
employed to keep him comfortable during his stay.

It took considerable effort on my part to get him to talk
about the operations of the new acquisition and what Chicago wanted him to do that week, because he no sooner got
going on any subject than he launched into another diatribe
against some real but mainly the imagined faults of the Italians.

Over the days I was with Henry, he became speechless at
the slightest slip of those around him: a delayed telephone

connection, a misplaced memo or file, or the late arrival of a "foreigner" to a meeting. I got the impression that he was obsessed with the trivial details of events.

Faced with the usual harmless Italian chaos that passes for their sense of order, whether at a bank, government office, or agency, he would become almost apoplectic with rage. He did not confine himself to groaning to me privately about it. He entered the fray with gusto, and could be seen gesticulating and shouting—in English!—just like an irate Italian at anybody he felt was guilty of being less than proper in manners or less than attentive to his needs. I'm sure he did not realize just how funny these scenes were and how ironic was his criticism of Italians when he was acting like one!

His total lack of empathy with the "foreigners" he was supposed to work with was dominating his entire life. He had forgotten what he was there for, which included getting on well with the local nationals who were to manage the subsidiary and integrate their operations into a Europe-wide business.

The amount of actual work he was required to do, including the review of previously negotiated financing and confirmation of partly concluded deals with suppliers in Turin and Milan, made up a busy schedule for anybody giving it their best shot. It was nearly impossible for somebody with neurotic attitudes toward the Italian people, individually and collectively.

In fact, I had to tell Chicago that his work rate was as bad as that of the Italians whom he criticized, because he spent so much time criticizing them and telling them how they did it much better in Illinois; and that neither he nor the people he was criticizing had much time left to do anything purposeful, except start over again where they last finished off with another bout of criticism.

A recall (with a generous early retirement) became inevitable. Henry did not fail because he was bad at his job as a manager of the buying function. He failed because he was not very good at being a foreigner!

All this does not mean, however, that you should refrain from criticizing the country you are in and go to the other extreme of criticizing the country that you are from. Your negotiating partners are likely to consider you disloyal and insincere if you attack your own country in tones normally reserved for attacking somebody else's. They will not regard you as other than fawning if you try to curry favor with them by behaving in such a way.

Franco wasn't funny

A colleague and I had occasion, not long after General Franco died, to negotiate with a shipper in Barcelona, Spain, who wanted to import specialized steels. He thought that there was a market for such products, and he believed (rightly) that the United States had a good reputation for technical excellence and sound quality in these particular steels.

Harry, my colleague, however, spent a lot of time at the evening meal late one night (and Spaniards, by the way, eat closer to midnight than to midday) knocking America.

It was not so much that Harry was knocking the country with which he expected the Catalonian importer to do business (this itself remarkably inept as a negotiating behavior) but that he was interspersing his derogatory remarks with fulsome and extravagant praise of Spain. "How wonderful it must be to live in Spain, and how I wish I had been brought up here," he said repeatedly.

We almost lost the deal for this impertinence. The fact was that our Spanish host had suffered considerably for many years at the hands of Franco's corrupt and bullying local party bosses, and this speech indicated to him that my colleague did not know what he was talking about. If Harry had lived under a fascist dictatorship instead of in a free country, he would have been more circumspect about criticizing America and praising Franco's Spain.

And on the aircraft home, Harry denounced the Spaniard for being ungrateful and giving us only a small first order. In the circumstances we were lucky to get even that.

Hence, be most careful how you behave as a foreigner. And get used to being one. In popular usage, a foreigner is somebody else; seldom do we see ourselves as foreigners, especially when we are abroad in another country.

Insensitivity

The apocryphal story of the Texan stopped for speeding in London deserves to be true. After a short conversation with the driver, the London policeman asked him, "Say, are you a foreigner?" To which the indignant Texan replied, "Certainly not! I'm American!"

Yet outside our own little backyards we are the foreigners. In fact we are foreigners to the vast bulk of the human race. We have the funny habits, the weird tastes, and the strange mannerisms, which is why tourists come to gawp at us and to mimic our oddities. When we leave our backyards and head for the rest of the world, we are the strangers in the lands of others; it is not their lands that are strange.

If you don't like foreigners, and cannot abide being one yourself, you are in the wrong business. In late-night wind-down sessions in bars and restaurants all over the world you will hear fellow negotiators from the United States, Britain, India, Pakistan, and Australia lay into the people they have been negotiating with that day, sometimes in the most patronizing, not to say racist, of ways. (Interestingly, though my sample is small, I have never heard derogatory remarks of

---

IVAN WAS NOT AMUSED

During a major negotiation with a Soviet trade delegation, the entire deal fell through due to the unfortunate remarks of one of the American participants to the senior Soviet trade official over a glass or two of vodka during an informal session.

The American negotiator apparently had very strong personal views on the political (in)competence of Ronald Reagan, and thought it appropriate to let his Soviet counterpart know how he felt about his country's president (presumably on the ground that because Mr. Reagan has a reputation of being anti-Communist he would be popular with the Soviet negotiators if he attacked the president in public).

As it happens, nothing worries Soviet officials, at all levels of their country's bureaucracy, more than attacks on persons in authority. They are notorious for getting nervous about criticism of their leaders emanating from their own citizens (and punish it severely), and are both worried and embarrassed when they hear such criticism from foreigners.

"He called his own president a poodle!" the Soviet negotiator told me privately. "Who would want to do serious business with somebody who speaks of his country's leaders in that way?" he added. Hence, they didn't.

---

this nature from South Africans, though I have heard them complain bitterly about people who abuse them in public yet insist on negotiating with them for business in private.)

Having discussed the subject with many Third World negotiators, though, I can identify the national group who most wantonly display their assumed superiority (with an arrogance bordering on racism): They are in fact citizens of the Soviet Union and other Eastern European Communist states.

This behavior does not endear them to the people they negotiate with in Third World countries, and it can boil over into open friction. Even the "fraternal" socialist regimes of Africa and Asia can become estranged by Great Russian nationalism posing as Soviet socialism. (I have no direct knowledge of how Cubans react to Soviet elitism, though I suppose it must irritate them too.)

Most negotiators, including the moaners mentioned above, manage to control their feelings overtly—most of the time!—during face-to-face sessions. Their inner feelings tend, however, to get aired, often in loud emotional voices, when they join the company of other expatriates in their hotels.

When their contempt for their opposite numbers is barely concealed, they are in great danger of not doing well in the negotiations. If offensive asides come across in contacts with people of the host nation or condescension leaks into their tones, they are bound to cause offense and in doing so, jeopardize their business.

Today there is extreme sensitivity across the globe to implicit, let alone explicit, affronts to national and personal pride. It may be that some of this sensitivity ought to be replaced with a sense of humor and a more sensible appreciation of the significance of those silly lapses in good manners (where they are lapses and not norms for behavior). Tired and emotional negotiators are boring wherever they come from, and so are their oversensitive victims. But beware, what for you can be passed off as a joke in bad taste might be enough in some parts of the world to get you jailed or deported (and perhaps worse).

We are the foreigners

For you, the need to appreciate your own foreignness is a precondition for entering the world of international business negotiating.

Consider two linked questions: Why do people live in different parts of the globe and not with you in your backyard? Why are they different from you? The answers are not trite, for they draw out essential truths that are no less important just because you take them for granted.

Different tribes of the human race live on different parts of the globe because their predecessors settled there and made a successful adaptation to local climatic and environmental circumstances.

They will pass on to their successors the most successful means for surviving on that part of the globe. In Greenland and northern Canada, the Inuit (Eskimos) survive by adapting to the environment. In Indonesia, locals do likewise. The same is true across the entire spectrum of weathers, seasons, soils, and sustenance.

Separating out that which is traditional and that which is modern (or international) in any society is a useful beginning for anybody contemplating a visit, especially someone with commercial business in mind. To the people who live in those parts, how they live and what adaptations they have made are perfectly natural and normal ways of behaving; so natural, in fact, that they regard your ignorance of them and their ways as a sign of *your* foreignness, not theirs.

Hence, I can be specific. In a strange land it is not the land that is strange, but you. You are the foreigner, not them. They live where they do because their predecessors discovered long ago how to live there successfully.

And in all cases it is not just a matter of climatic adaptation—the cultural, historical, and political backgrounds have also influenced the local approach to business.

The American who negotiates in Tokyo in much the same way as he does in Chicago will end up having to look for business elsewhere. The German who ships his goods to Egypt because his Arab counterpart said yes to his proposition might have to send them back again.

Pace the negotiations too fast in one culture and you'll get nothing for your pains, pace them too slow in another and you'll be beaten by the competition.

These kinds of negotiating errors are caused by forgetting your foreignness. You are on your own, perhaps thousands of miles from the part of the world that is most familiar to you, and you are bound to feel a trifle uneasy with your unfamiliar surroundings. You must realize, of course, that it is you that is unfamiliar, not the surroundings, for they have been there a long time.

So, if your foreignness leads you into error, you must invest some time and energy in compensating for it. You should make an effort to find out about the people with whom you want to do business.

You could do worse than starting by learning a few of the polite greetings and salutations in the language of the country you intend to visit. If you are likely to spend any period of time in residence there you should be able to make your stomach an ally in the cause of learning and introduce yourself to at least restaurant-level competence in the language.

Making an effort in this way will show your counterpart that you are less of a foreigner than someone who has not the slightest clue about the country's language. Becoming less of a foreigner is a small first step toward showing respect for the people with whom you want to do business, and from mutual respect more than one good deal will follow.

If you are not yet convinced of this, you have already forgotten what Henry should have remembered: The worst thing you can do when negotiating abroad is forget that you are the foreigner.

ANSWERS TO SELF-ASSESSMENT TEST 1

1 There are three foreigners at the meeting: you and your two colleagues from corporate headquarters. The eight Chinese citizens are local nationals and not foreigners.

> **If you answered "three" add 10 points; for any other answer deduct 10 points (and read chapter 1!).**

2 a Not if you wish to develop a proper negotiating relationship with them. You have no idea of their views on the law (perhaps they support similar laws in France). It is best not to criticize your own country when abroad.   (−10)

  b The very most you should ever do if you must comment at all, being particularly careful to inform them objectively rather than indicating your own views.   (3)

  c Good avoidance move. Keeps you out of trouble and could be followed by *e* if you are pushed further.   (5)

  d Safest move if you suspect the matter is controversial and are not sure of your hosts' views.   (10)

  e Good for stalling and gets them talking and you listening.   (10)

3 a It is always pointless to criticize the customs of another country to a stranger. He could be a Western-educated Arab who sounds like an American, and he might deeply resent what he regards as your ignorance or rudeness. How a country organizes its affairs is none of your business, particularly if you really want to do any with them.   (−10)

  b Always the best policy. Airports and bars are full of wise guys who resent the countries they are in and people who live differently from themselves. They can get you into trouble and will bore you once they get your attention. Ignore them and their silly comments.   (10)

SELF-ASSESSMENT TEST 2

1 You are about to leave home for a ten-day selling trip to five major Canadian cities. Do you:

a Select enough clothes from your wardrobe to last the ten days, plus some extras in case you need them?
b Travel light, with what you stand up in, plus a single change of garments?
c Compromise between having every contingency covered and having no contingencies covered?

2 You run a consultancy in new technology and receive a telex inviting you to speak to a trade conference in Acapulco, Mexico. They ask for your fee and terms for participating. Do you:

a Go at a nominal fee since you have not been to Mexico before and would like to visit Acapulco?
b Quote your standard fee and terms, and include first-class air travel?
c Ask them how many participants will be attending and what they are paying per head?

3 You are flying to Sydney and get into conversation with a businessman in the next seat who is going as far as Hawaii. He asks where you are staying in Sydney and you reply, "The place I always stay, the Regent at Circular Key." He advises you of a "beautiful hotel, the Corroboree" he has discovered at the "back of Kings Cross" and waxes on eloquently about it until the plane arrives in Hawaii. Before leaving he tells you to mention his name and introduce yourself to the hotel's owners, Ben and Peggy, and assures you it's an excellent place to stay. On arriving in Sydney do you:

a Take a look at the Corroboree?
b Take a taxi to the Regent?

CHAPTER **2**

The Business of Travel—or, If You Enjoy It You're Obviously a Tourist

No romance here

Business travel is seldom romantic or exciting for those who often undertake it. Professional international negotiators regard travel as a chore that must be endured because it is a necessary part of the job. The suitcase life is by no means as glamorous as the stay-at-homes believe it to be. Those who suffer from crushed shirts or blouses, creased pants or skirts, and stale socks or stockings are unimpressed by the travel fantasies of those who do not.

Traveling occasionally as a tourist is all very well (and economical) if it is a prelude to spending two weeks soaking up a lazy tan on a beach somewhere, but traveling regularly on business is an entirely different activity, especially when you have to perform brilliantly on arrival halfway around the world.

Travel itself is a chore whatever mode of transport you choose. Traveling first or business class, instead of on a tourist cheapie, reduces the burden somewhat but does not eliminate it entirely. Jet lag does not defer to the class of travel that you use (quite the opposite, in fact, if you overindulge in the "free" booze offered in first and business class).

Overseas travel costs you more than the fare you pay. You suffer the inconvenience of the journey to and from the airports you fly from and to, the boredom of the flights in between and perhaps the follies of the hotels at which you stay.

Announcing your first visit to Hawaii to your friends may cause them to feel envious of your job, but if you arrive in Honolulu tired, dehydrated, and in a rainstorm, collapse into a bedroom that is next to a noisy air-conditioning shaft, and find that your luggage has been lost somewhere en route and that your dearest wish is to sleep when you should be meeting the people you have come to see, you may decide that the experience is less than glamorous.

On your tenth visit to Hawaii (whatever you tell the guys in the office) you will view the long journey to get there with something less than enthusiasm, knowing that it will take just as long to get back. By your twentieth visit you will very likely feel it is time that somebody else undertook the chore.

Chore or not, there is no way that international business can be conducted without travel. The telephone is no substitute, nor is the telex, facsimile, video, or satellite hookup. Sending a letter is not much better. You can effect an introduction by mail, even make them an offer, but you cannot really negotiate a complex deal, particularly if the option of getting off your backside and going out to see them is available. Bargaining without visual contact and close physical presence is a risky business when the stakes are high and the issues aren't routine.

Long-haul travel automatically involves air travel, and this means incarceration in a large cylinder that tunnels through the sky in eight- to ten-hour shifts (the airlines call them "legs"). This need not induce serenity and peace. In addition to the squawking kids three rows along and the drunk next to you (or *vice versa*), there is always the irritation of other people sitting between you and the cabin service.

A TICKET IS NOT A SEAT

Ticketing is an art form. Ordering an air ticket is only the first step toward getting onto the aircraft. They still have to get the tickets into your hands, which can be easier said than done.

I once ordered a ticket for a flight from New York to Nairobi, which had not arrived by the day before my journey. The agency assured me that they had sent it to me in Connecticut the same day I ordered it. Despite several phone calls about the missing ticket they did not mention by which means they had sent it and I assumed it was via U.S. mail. In the end I faced having to purchase another ticket from a local agent at full fare and in desperation, called my head office in Boston in case it had been sent to them. Sure enough, my ticket had been there for a week!

Getting your ticket and yourself to the airport does not necessarily get you on an aircraft, either. The airlines reserve the "right" (it's outright impudence, in fact!) to overbook each flight. This could leave you standing at the check-in with your travel plans in ruins.

I was denied boarding at Amman, Jordan, because the check-in computer said the plane was full, even though I was obviously the first passenger in the line. After my vigorous protests and much confusion, they discovered a computer malfunction: It had listed every seat as being occupied by the same passenger, a Mr. O'Shaughnessy—a cousin of the famous Mr. Murphy?—who in any event didn't even turn up!

You could even get on the aircraft and still get thrown off.

I witnessed a woman being put off an aircraft about to depart for New Zealand, although she had been issued a boarding pass and allowed on with the rest of the passengers, because the airline did not discover it was overbooked until there was one passenger left standing after everybody else had sat down. Thank goodness she was not Miss World, or they might have thrown me off instead! Moral: If you get on board, get seated, strapped in, and stuck into your newspaper, and don't look up until takeoff.

On a long-haul flight (say, the twenty hours to Sydney from London) you learn the difference between a jumbo with 315 people on board and one that is more than half empty. On a full plane, the service grinds slowly toward you or arrives just as you have got to sleep; it is a law of travel that no matter where you sit, the cabin service always starts somewhere else!

The best you can do is to make your entire journey as comfortable as possible. This means going first or business class. Money is never "saved" by going economy or tourist class. If you are more tired than you need to be because you tried to skimp on the airfare, it could cost your company more than the money they "save" sending you economy.

On lugging your luggage

The next target for your attention ought to be your luggage. Most people take far too much with them, and the more they take the more they have to carry and be responsible for.

Why business negotiators traveling, not to the outposts of Ogoland, where little of what they might need is available to them, but to the richer parts of the globe, pack enough shirts to change more than once a day and enough suits and accessories to last an entire season baffles me, though it was an apparent stroke of ill luck that woke me up to the idiocy of these ways.

On a flight to London my luggage was lost. Naturally, I was not very pleased with this occurrence and waxed long and loudly on the theme of changing the airport's name from Heathrow to Thiefrow, which could have offended the good men and women of London's busiest airport, but I hope that they put my wild allegations down to jet lag and the time in the morning.

I had only the fairly crumpled suit and shirt I was wearing, and my first appointment was in two hours. What to do? Obviously I had to acquire some replacement clothes. And this opened my eyes. There are hundreds of places to buy inexpensive clothes in cities like London. A quick visit to a clothing store will soon produce a most presentable outfit.

The question occurred to me: Why do I insist on carrying all this luggage around, risking my health and temperament, when I can purchase what I need on arrival?

The answer eventually became a way of life for me when I travel. I decided there and then to travel light, replacing anything I have not brought with a quick purchase locally.

For a two-week trip you are unlikely to need anything more than what you can get into a regulation-size cabin bag (21 × 16 × 8 inches). Women should note that they have the privilege of being able to add their handbags to the cabin bag allowance. This suggests that they should take a large handbag. Men should stuff their pockets with odds and ends.

If after you pack your cabin bag you find that you want to take more possessions, I suggest that you are taking too much. Empty it out and be more ruthless.

I have found it useful to wear my business suit jacket onto the plane with a pair of lightweight casual pants. My suit pants are neatly folded in the bag. Once on the plane, I neatly fold my suit jacket into the overhead locker. On one business trip around Europe I appeared neatly turned out at all times using combinations of three pairs of lightweight pants and a single blazer—dark pants for more formal sessions and light pants for relaxation.

The rest of the bag is for accessories. What I take I wash and iron at the hotel (of which more in a moment) and if I need something else I simply buy it locally.

If you are unconvinced of the virtues of this policy, ask yourself what you intend to do with all the shirts and underwear you insist on carrying. Are you intending to spend your trip lugging around a pile of dirty laundry? If you balk at carrying dirty clothes, you must intend to get them cleaned as you go and if this is the case, you can cut down on the number of shirts or blouses by using the same-day service at your hotels. Clothes sent for cleaning in the morning are ready for you by 6 P.M. (or you are in the wrong hotel!).

It's better to send a steady stream of single items to the cleaners rather than pile them together to make a load. You never know when an emergency might strike and you'll need a quick change. Accidentally spilled soup or booze, a sudden tear, or an unexpected invitation to dinner or an appointment can catch you unprepared if your only other clothes are waiting to go to the laundry.

You can buy low-priced shirts and such almost anywhere to supplement what you have brought. I am sometimes asked what happens if you buy locally and then have to carry it all home. That depends on whether you want to take it home. You can throw items away!

Why balk at throwing away a cheap shirt you wore only once for a specific purpose connected with your business when you think nothing of spending five or more times what the shirt cost on a meal or entertainment? Both activities are related to your business, and you should be philosophical rather than neurotic about their worth.

On the toiletries front the same rules apply. True, you can get an ingenious adapter that enables you to take electrical appliances with you and use them almost anywhere in the world. You can also get battery versions of shavers, curlers, hairdryers, and toothbrushes. But why carry them with you when you risk losing them en route or having them fail for some reason?

Everything you need in the way of soaps, shampoos, perfumes, aftershaves, talcs, hairsprays, and toothpaste, including simple throwaway razors and toothbrushes, is always available at hotel shops, so why carry it? You can carry an emergency supply if your security level bothers you, but make sure it is a miniature supply and not enough to see you through a long prison sentence.

As for towels and facecloths, you have no reason to assume

that your hotel will not have them freely available (unless these are for you what child psychologists call security blankets). Of course, in some parts of the world it would be unsafe to expect to find accessories freely available, but in Europe, Australia, Japan, Latin America, and South Africa, it is silly to pay for hotel services that include towels and so forth and still insist on lugging your own around as well.

Naturally, your bag will contain your business papers, and these should also be kept to a minimum. Whatever your intentions, it is unlikely that you will work through as many of your office papers as you think on your journey. I am not at all convinced that you should take your office work with you anyway. It is a delusion of the busy (read disorganized) executive to believe that he or she will use the flight time and the evenings in the hotel to sort through company budget accounts, reports from other sections, quotations for other contracts, and overdue reports for the boss.

The truth is (and I have checked this by asking executives to be candid about their use of time on overseas trips) that you will only half-heartedly look at those office papers during the flight, and you will probably be too tired to look at them in the evenings. And if you do look at them you will only worry about the obvious things that should be done and waste a lot of time thinking about not being able to do them. Mostly, the papers will only add weight to your luggage.

A major advantage of the single regulation-size cabin bag on an international trip is that you eliminate at a stroke the anxiety of searching the baggage claim area for your other suitcases (another law of business travel says that your luggage is never the first off the plane). Waiting for your bags can add an hour to your journey time at most airports, especially when two or three jumbos are decanting their luggage into the same space.

Apart from the risk of your luggage being mislaid, it can be stolen. Some victims of theft ask for it. If you display your affluence by using well-known credit card luggage labels you ought not to complain if thieves make a beeline for the obvious jackpot.

With hand baggage only, you are bound to be among the first through customs and immigration and first to the taxis. You should be booking into your hotel while the rest of them are lugging their suitcases up the ramps to the customs hall. You could be showering, or sampling a Martini by the poolside, while they are fighting for a taxi and joining the mob scene at reception.

Hotels

Hotels are another fact of business life for the international negotiator. They can either help or hinder you on your trip, so the best advice is not to skimp on them in a futile search for economies. Where you can you should stay in the four- or five-star type, preferably one that is part of an international hotel chain (Hyatt, Hilton, Inter-Continental, Holiday Inn, Sheraton, Marriott, Westin, and so on).

My reason for advising this is quite simple; you know what you are getting for what you pay in the chain hotel. A negotiator does not have time for cultural immersion on a business trip. He or she does not have time to seek out the quaint and the ethnic during the few hours available for bed and relaxation. It is best to trust to the familiar rather than risk the unfamiliar. Tips from people who stayed at this or that unusual hostelry off the beaten track should seldom be trusted and even less often acted upon—if it is that good they should keep it to themselves!

The advice of old hands can often be useful, but be warned that the world's aircraft are full of people who like to give the impression that they are old hands in this or that place. Their ideas on what constitutes good service or adequate plumbing will more than likely qualify them for a Ph.D. in

TAXI!

A word, by way of warning, about airport taxi ripoffs. They must be avoided at all costs. Most airports have prominently displayed notices warning visitors not to get into anything other than an official taxi, and the local police often take the view that if you ignore specific warnings the consequences are none of their business.

At some airports they even hand out printed warnings about taxi crooks to visitors as they move through immigration, but still these are ignored by some of the "it won't happen to me" brigade.

Many years ago, while passing through Colombo, in what has since been renamed Sri Lanka, I was ripped off by a taxi driver who pretended to know the person I was supposed to be meeting; he told me, would you believe, that he had been sent to pick me up by this person! It cost me the equivalent of a month's wages for a Sri Lankan laborer for the ride, but it taught me to avoid the swindlers who plague every airport I've been in since.

People who ignore the warnings are damn fools. The police will not come to your rescue (except if physical violence is involved) when it comes to paying the charge. At most you might haggle the price downwards a little, but if you haggle with taxi swindlers why did you get into the mess in the first place?

In some cities you can do a deal with a licensed taxi driver, however. You will be offered a half- or quarter-price run to the airport providing you let him take more than one fare (in Greece, taxis always used to seek more than one fare, before the socialist government made it illegal, often without asking you). I agreed to this on one occasion in New York, and the driver went off to look for another customer at the air terminal. Unfortunately he was unable to find anybody wanting to go out to Kennedy at that time. But a deal being a deal (after all, he was a New York cabbie) he took me to Kennedy off the meter for a flat fare of six dollars.

eccentricity. They may not require first-class telephone links and top-rate reception services.

A chain hotel has the capacity to put things right if something is wrong. A Sheraton in Connecticut once changed my room merely because I mentioned to reception that the television was not working properly, while Hyatt, in San Francisco, gave me a suite instead of a room because they took so long to pick me up at the airport.

Negotiators working away from their home base need good communications, and this means plenty of phone or telex lines (preferably with direct dialing facilities) at your disposal. Watch those hotel charges for calls, though—they are positively lethal unless you negotiate a standard telephone company rate for all your calls, which you can do if you regularly use an international chain for your hotel requirements.

Never underestimate the value of a decent phone service. It used to be nearly impossible to do business in France because of its phone system. Instant access to your office or your home can be a soothing balm when you are under pressure. Small hotels have inadequate phone facilities. Some have phones in the hall, not in the room, which can be off-putting when you have confidential business to discuss. Recently, I was prevented from getting my office to do a credit check on a client in upcountry Australia because the phone was not just in the hall, it was within earshot of the bar where my client was sitting sipping his beer!

Hotel chains tend to be more secure from the attentions of thieves. How much you worry about theft depends on what you are carrying and when you were last a victim of crime. If you have never experienced theft of your possessions you will probably not take precautions, until some unknown thief educates you. Remember, there is nothing sacred about your wallet or passport or handbag.

In a different environment you may unwisely relax about things because you never worry about them at home. I know a copper buyer who had his trousers stolen on his first night in Zambia, but the thief left behind his wallet which was on the dressing table. Sir Geoffrey Howe, the British foreign minister, had his pants and their contents (one hundred dollars) stolen from his locked sleeping compartment on a train traveling at one hundred miles an hour across normally law-abiding Britain!

Thieves steal things in order to sell them. Your business papers will probably be dumped as worthless (unless the theft is aimed at industrial espionage or the nature of your papers leads to an opportunistic bit of the same). Hence, separate your papers from your suitcase, although beware of the risks in doing so.

I stayed at the Post House, Heathrow, London the week that it opened and placed my papers by the bed. When I returned at midnight I found that my possessions, such as they were, had been removed and incinerated by the maid, who thought that I had checked out since she could see no luggage in the room. The management groveled profusely, of course, and I (or rather they) had to replace my shirt, socks, and pants before breakfast, but I had to work without my papers and notes for the rest of the week.

In sum, be security conscious. Lock your door. Use the peephole in the door to check who is knocking. Place valuables in the hotel safe and generally make it difficult for thieves to get at your possessions. They will prefer to spend their time liberating the possessions of those who are careless with them.

Twenty cents is no ripoff

Another advantage of a chain hotel is that they generally provide, at a price of course, banking services. I know that they charge for these, especially when changing currency, but I doubt whether the percentage differences in currency charges are really worth the fuss that some people make about them. A couple of cents per pound sterling might matter if you are changing several thousand dollars, but hardly make a difference for a twenty-dollar bill.

For some people, getting two centimes to the dollar less from the hotel bank than you can get downtown appears to cause more heartache (and longer boring speeches at the bar) than the 50 percent markup on the bar bill. I've seen supposedly serious negotiators reduced to grievous apoplexy over an alleged currency ripoff at reception, involving perhaps the loss of fifty cents in total across the entire transaction. Yet these same "business professionals" will willingly pay the same hotel fifteen dollars for a bottle of wine that costs two in the local supermarket.

If they ever thought about the markup they pay on hotel food (I've heard it can be over 4000 percent in some places) they might take a more relaxed view of the "ripoffs" in the *bureau de change* and more important, they might spare us all the dubious benefits of listening to their outrage.

In summary then, this is my advice to the business traveler about to embark on his or her first 100,000 miles:

- Fly first or business class on all trips. If your company argues, you are working for the wrong company.
- Restrict your luggage to a single carry-on cabin bag (plus a handbag if you are a woman or full pockets if you are a man).
- Stay only at international chain hotels.
- Praise every display of good service and suggest a remedy for any letdown you experience.
- Reduce jet lag by adjusting your watch to the local time of the country you are visiting, avoiding alcoholic drink on flight but taking plenty of other liquids, and going to bed only when the locals do.

- Use only official taxis, keep your valuables in a safe place, and if held up by a mugger give him what he wants without arguing. Your life is worth more than whatever possessions you are carrying.

ANSWERS TO SELF-ASSESSMENT TEST 2

1 **a** This must be your first trip; otherwise you would have more sense.   (−10)
 b By far the most sensible choice. Light travelers have less to worry about, get off the plane and through customs quicker, find it easier to make their way from hotel to airport, and can get around the airport much more easily.   (10)
 c Better perhaps than *a*, but it depends on toward which end of the spectrum you compromise.   (5)

2 **a** You are not a serious business negotiator if you allow your personal desires to interfere with your commercial judgment. If you rationalize this answer right through, you will probably do the trip for nothing or, worse, offer to pay half your costs just to get to Mexico!   (−20)
 b Clearly you are not intimidated by the alleged romance of exotic places, though you ought to ask for details first, as in *c*.   (5)
 c Much better. The more information you acquire, the better. They may fill a stadium with people wanting to know about new technology, and your rate could work out at two cents per head, making your fee look ridiculous.   (10)

3 **a** Advice about local hotels is almost always not worth acting upon. If the Corroboree is not to your taste you have the hassle of moving out. Ben and Peggy may have suited your companion, but may be a pain in the neck to you.   (−10)
 b Always your best bet if you are satisfied with the hotel you normally use (and you should be happy at the Sydney Regent, but don't take my word for it!).   (10)

SELF-ASSESSMENT TEST 3

1 Your company is anxious to develop overseas markets for its high-technology products. A Soviet representative invites you to Moscow to discuss a possible contract to supply a complete production system. Which of the following is likely to be the most difficult point to negotiate in the opening sessions?

a Price
b Technical specifications
c Delivery
d Performance standards
e Export licenses
f Methods of payment

2 Your opposite number from the Soviet negotiating team is polite but otherwise cool. Do you:

a Try to develop a personal relationship?
b Treat him with respect but keep your distance?

3 The Soviet negotiator tells you that they are having parallel negotiations with your major competitors, and you know this to be true because your rivals are using the same hotel and restaurants as you. He insists on price concessions from you to match those offered by the competition. Do you:

a Agree if it still leaves the deal with a profit?
b Decline unless your prices can take a cut?
c Offer some other concession instead?
d Refuse to budge on price?

CHAPTER **3**

Negotiating with the (Russian) Comrades—or, Safety in Buck-Passing

The monopoly of foreign trade

Trading with Communist countries is as different as a hammer is from a sickle, and there is no way you can get into this relatively lucrative activity in the same way that you would break into the European market. It is therefore a useful place to begin the main part of this book.

For a start, the Soviets do not believe (officially at least) in the free market (or free much else), and they will certainly cast a jaundiced eye over you at Sheremetyevo airport, Moscow, if you turn up on a speculative visit hoping to sell a million gross of tappet holes to the manager of the local dynamo factory.

The Soviet market is not like any you have dealt with in the West, and you could save yourself a lot of trouble by finding out just how different it is before you get your visa from Ivan, your local Soviet consul; don't wait until you are slurping your borscht in Leningrad.

To put it simply, the Soviet state jealously guards its monopoly of foreign trade, and everything, but everything, must go through official and bureaucratic channels. Nothing is imported or exported at the whims of individuals, be they ever so powerful. The system of control is all-pervasive, and there is precious little hope of getting around it with the usual dodges used by those in a hurry to enrich themselves. You will bend to the Soviet system of the state monopoly of foreign trade or you will not trade with them at all. It's as simple and as brutal as that.

If a manager in the Soviet or Eastern European socialist system wants to acquire machinery for some purpose connected with the planned output targets assigned to his plant, he doesn't simply check the catalogues of suppliers of such machinery, invite them to send proposals, and then meet with their sales personnel for preliminary discussions. And even if for some reason he did do it this way, he could not initiate a purchase by opening negotiations with the supplier while clearing the finance with his board of directors. He has to go through channels.

All industrial and commercial decisions are subject to planning at the top and in the absence of a market, all decisions are made by bureaucratic means in the numerous administrative levels that plan, manage, and review all economic activity in the Soviet Union.

Industrial ministries supervise the work of product groups and their associated research and development projects, and state committees coordinate overlapping interests and developments. To acquire imports of machinery and such, these organizations must work through the Ministry of Foreign Trade, which operates foreign trade organizations (FTOs) parallel with the industrial ministries and, in some cases, major industrial plants.

The negotiating process between the Western supplier and the actual end user of its products has to work through these numerous levels of decision making and various strands of the bureaucratic system of ministries, state committees, and

FTOs. You cannot short-circuit the system and go straight to the end user for a decision to buy. Indeed, it is unusual for a supplier ever to meet with the end user (which creates its own complications, as we shall see).

Have you got the picture? Well, just to confuse matters, the system changes regularly, the extent to which its strictures and procedures are applied vary, and experience shows that on occasion the system will leap over normal sequences and produce a "quick" decision. Since you will never know when this is likely to happen or why (perhaps somebody is covering for somebody else who, back along the line, has made a foul-up of some kind), you ought not to rely on it happening to you.

Getting business from the Soviets

There are various ways in which you might get into trading with Communist states. You could be a subcontractor to a Western supplier who holds a contract with the relevant Soviet department. If you are, your negotiating will be confined to the deal you make with the major contractor, but some aspects of their requirements will reflect the nature of their deal with the Soviets. You might find that they require considerable technical detail from you; this is a feature of Soviet-type contracts.

You might be approached by a representative of a Soviet trade mission (STM). Soviet specialists constantly sift through the technical press and attend exhibitions, launches, presentations, and so on. They look for products that might match Soviet needs. They also act as the official link between you and the end user. They might supervise the entire negotiation or merely introduce you to the next layer of principals in the bureaucracy they represent.

Another way into the Soviet market is via the services of an agent specializing in Communist markets. He finds a Soviet or an Eastern European manufacturer who is looking for a machine to do a particular job and matches it with your company's products. He may initiate the inquiry with you on speculation or act as a searcher of business for you on regular tours of potential customers. For this service, and for carrying you through the process of negotiation, which could last anything up to two years, he would get a percentage of the gross value of the order (say, 4.5 percent).

You could also send a representative as part of a delegation touring the Soviet Union and Eastern Europe, perhaps organized by your trade association, or you could exhibit at a trade fair.

The one thing you are most unlikely to do is to wander around the Soviet Union at will, looking for business, as you might wander around Germany or Brazil.

Technical obsessions

Soviet trade negotiators are professionals, not enthusiastic amateurs. They prepare thoroughly and are well briefed, and their internal systems compel them to act in ways that force you to disclose a great deal more than is normal in Western negotiations, especially in the technical aspects of the products involved.

The obsession of Soviet negotiators with technical data is not surprising if the industrial and political structure of their society is taken into account.

In the absence of price and competition as indicators and regulators of quality, it is necessary for something else to take these roles; otherwise resources would be mismatched and inputs chosen arbitrarily. Communist societies replace the market as the arbitrator of demand and supply with committees of bureaucrats using various output indicators (tons, meters, cubic volumes, and so on) in place of monetary values, though they do not always by any means totally avoid the mismatch of resources to needs and their economies can be very inefficient as a result.

Soviet officials are charged with checking the suitability, reliability, and quality of purchases, and they take full responsibility for their decisions. Hence, they are careful; they respond not to hunches and entrepreneurial initiatives but are risk-averse and routine-minded. In other words, they check everything and require evidence for their records that they have checked everything, and these records can be used to check on them by other committees whose sole job is to see that everything has been checked by those reporting to them.

Your negotiations are likely to be divided into two main stages: first, the assessment of the technical competence of the product you are selling and what commitments they can extract from you in these qualifying negotiations; and second, the negotiations on the terms under which you will trade.

Great care is needed by negotiators in both phases, because while the Soviet state is a "good payer," as bankers put it, there is a caveat to their soundness as debtors: They pay promptly only if the terms of the contract are strictly met by the supplier.

If you accept loose terms in the performance negotiations you may live to regret their literal interpretation by faceless bureaucrats or end users at a later stage. The Soviet official regards the contract as a sacred document and will operate it to the letter if it suits his interests.

For example, if you say your machine can work under any temperature because you have never heard of a problem arising from the temperature range common to your own country, remember that some bureaucrat in an office in Omsk, on the basis of what he considers is a contractual obligation, may send your machines to a factory in Yakutsk, deep in Siberia. If your product freezes at twenty below zero and stops a production line, which prevents that plant from meeting its quotas (or plausibly can be blamed for doing so), he will demand recompense; and nobody claiming compensation ever asks for small amounts! So if your payments are held up while you explain what you meant by "any temperature," don't forget to kick yourself for being careless.

Get the contract right

The worst thing you can do is oversell your product to a Communist bureaucrat. They are held mercilessly liable for their own contractual agreements as state suppliers to end users. You can get an idea of the standard Soviet attitude to performance contracts from this statement by one supplier in the aircraft industry in respect to his customers: "After considerable negotiations with the customer as to what will be produced, the designer signs the contract and symbolically hands over his testicles with the contract. When the aircraft is delivered as specified, he gets his testicles back."

All their negotiators are committee men and women brought up in a world where everything they do is covered by paperwork, and they won't do much for you unless they get it all written down. If you are careless with your commitments you might as well hand over whatever is for you the biological equivalent of your testicles.

Failure to deliver as promised (whether in time, quality, or quantity) is endemic in the Soviet bureaucratic economy, and much time is spent by managers and their "fixers" tirading against each other's failures and attempting to shift the blame elsewhere. This is where paperwork is worth its weight in buck-passing.

If there was an open legal system in the USSR, lawyers would be making small, and not so small, fortunes suing for alleged breaches of contract all over Soviet industry; and

ON-SITE INSPECTION? NOT IN THIS COUNTRY, COMRADE!

A Detroit manufacturer of welding equipment was surprised to receive a large bill from a Soviet customer for the repair of some of its machines. Not only was the charge excessive—you could almost buy the equipment new for that price—but the alleged fault had been identified by the manufacturer's own engineers many years previously as one caused by operator misuse.

In subsequent discussions with the Soviet foreign trade organization responsible for the end user's product group, the U.S. negotiators insisted on the source of the problem. They drew their counterparts' attention to the extremely detailed operating manual that specifically warned against certain operator practices and explained what would happen unless the operators followed the precise instructions when switching off the equipment.

This was to no avail. The Soviet officials pressed for penalty payments under the terms of the original contract and insisted that the repair costs were not excessive.

In response to this deadlock, the U.S. team insisted on inspecting the equipment. This was immediately denied by the Soviet negotiators, on the grounds that there was nothing in the contract about on-site inspection.

The Americans refused to pay for repairs that they disputed, especially when they were denied access for inspection by their own engineers.

The problem lay in the contract terms. Unless a contract specifies on-site inspection in cases of dispute it is unlikely that the Soviet officials will vary its terms retrospectively. Their total sensitivity about on-site inspection in the arms negotiations will be replicated in commercial dealings unless you insist on it from the start.

Remember: What you sign you live with—or without, as the case may be.

whereas there are other than monetary sanctions on Comrade Ivan, against you they have a financial one. If they don't have that for some reason, under their state monopoly of all trade they have the final one of total exclusion from their markets, forever.

So get your performance contract precisely right. Specify exactly what your product can do and make no commitments that you cannot be absolutely sure your product can deliver on. Under no circumstances slip in "extras" that well-stocked American engineering departments could cope with, but which might be beyond actual Soviet practice in less well stocked or outright primitive plants run by crews who are less than enthusiastic about standards, particularly if they are not well motivated under their payments systems.

On their side of the table they will bring in high-quality engineers to go over your product's specifications, most with names as confusing to remember as those in Tolstoy's novels, each representing some bureaucratic interest in their confusing management structures.

It is no good saying that you have explained it all before and they can refer to the previous committee for details; your listeners will have come from a different interest group and will not be impressed or influenced by the statements of administrative units several layers or several structures away from their own. (Think of it from their point of view. The other bunch may drop them in the proverbial fertilizer, so they must check for themselves before they sign anything at their level.)

You must therefore be prepared for repetitive and intensive bouts of explanation, promotion, and negotiation on technical aspects of your products, perhaps over several months, and you must not get wearied by this exhausting procedure. If it does weary you, try another market!

If you are not technically qualified to submit to searching interrogations on your product's performance—and sometimes your questioners will seem like off-duty staff from the KGB's Lubyanka prison—you must get a technical specialist from your company sent along with you.

Penalty clauses

This point is especially important when you are negotiating penalty clauses, which can be seen as the individual Soviet bureaucrat's insurance policy against being held responsible for failures; with a battery of penalty clauses general enough to cover almost everything that can go wrong, he can cover himself against criticism and protect his job (which at his level will accord him and his family important privileges).

The Soviet negotiator will try to get a penalty clause inserted that protects him against you not delivering on time. You should hold back any startling concessions on this point and should certainly avoid a commitment to deliver to the site in the Soviet Union on time, as you are in the hands of foreign seamen, foreign dockers, and foreign railways, all of them influenced by the Communists. Delivery should either be ex works (yours, not theirs), to the gates of a U.S. port or, as a last resort, alongside a Soviet dock.

If you recklessly show signs of weakness here (i.e., concede too much too fast), they might try for a penalty clause for failing to send the associated documentation to them! And why not? This bureaucrat is concerned more with paperwork than the actual goods, which are a problem for some other bureaucrat.

But the penalties will not stop there, if they can force you to concede more. The engineers who are concerned with the goods will require their negotiators to enforce a penalty for any delays in commissioning their plant.

Beware: You may not be solely responsible for when these plants are commissioned, though your contract might imply

this. The Soviet system uses ranks of inspectors who special-
ize in checking on everything, including each other—sometimes, even on the parts that are preassembled inside the
machine (they might insist that you strip it down, even when
the parts are sealed in!). You can rapidly commit your company to all kinds of penalties or other pressures by ill-consid-
ered concessions on commissioning dates.

The problem of inspection can be partly obviated by having their inspectors visit your plant to do some of their work
while the machinery is under assembly. In this case you must
make the Soviets responsible for the travel and subsistence
costs of their inspectors.

Soviet inspectors require an excessive quantity of documentation related to imports. So much is required that it creates a suspicion that it is to be used for other purposes, such
as unauthorized (that is, unpaid for) transfer of Western technology.

They will want detailed workshop drawings (including
part assembly and mountings), lists of parts (down to wash-
ers and bolts), the test procedures and how they are to be
conducted, certificates of the materials used (even chemical and other analyses), photographs of the plant (from all
angles and not just those supplied in your brochures), full
technical specifications of everything (and they mean *everything*), full maintenance manuals (in Russian if they can get
them), detailed information—including drawings—on parts
that are expected to wear out, and certificates for welding
and other work not open to test once the equipment is delivered.

In return for this plethora of detail, they will be less than
efficient in getting information to you from their side, particularly on the end user's requirements or operating conditions.
There is not a lot you can do about this other than wait, having made certain that your contractual obligations on delivery dates are not triggered until you receive essential details
from them and are suspended if there are delays emanating

from their side. Do not underestimate the problems of delays caused by the Soviets themselves. These are legendary. Technical specifications arrive later than promised; their inspectors turn up two weeks after they were supposed to have left their own country; they leave a week before they should, with parts coming off the line that they were meant to inspect, and so on.

You are bound to be fairly confident in making a penalty commitment in the area of reaching promised quality and quantity targets. After all, you are in the business of supplying high-quality products. You should, however, be able to anticipate the negotiating line that will often be taken by the buyer (and not just a Soviet one): "If the quality and quantity claims you make for your machines are true, you will have no reason to fear agreeing to a penalty clause if these promises are not met."

It could be game, set, and match if you fall for this without being very sure to have precise responsibilities demarcated. You should guarantee the quality and quantity levels of output (and things like energy consumption, waste levels, and noise or emission levels) from your machines if and only if the inputs are of a very closely specified quality (which they must guarantee to you), the operators are fully competent and properly trained (which they must also guarantee to you), and the general working environment is suitable (which they must agree to provide).

At the very least, you will require site inspection rights of your machines and how they are used in normal working sessions—for your engineers, not theirs. And you had better get it agreed what is meant by a normal working session if you are required to guarantee performance for a time period. You might assume single-shift five-day work weeks and give a two-year guarantee, only to discover later, when parts are worn out, that they are working three shifts over six days (fairly standard practice), thereby decreasing the duration of any performance guarantee you give.

WHO'S SORRY NOW?

The Soviet fad for penalty clauses is not bounded by any consideration for who might be to blame for the failure to reach promised (and perhaps normal) performance standards. Unless, that is, you specifically insist on qualifying your promises with a clause in the contract to exclude your liability if the failing is in any way connected with the user's practices.

Legal experts on Soviet contracting practice suggest that something like the following be included in the contract that you sign. If it isn't, you ought not to sign—if you do you should file your contract in the I'm-going-to-be-sorry drawer!

(We) warrant that the technical documentation to be supplied will permit the licensee to manufacture, to the extent and under the conditions herein stated, products having the characteristics specified in the Schedule (attached) provided that (a) licensee complies with all technical standards, instructions and recommendations from licensor; (b) the machinery, tools and equipment used by the licensee are in conformity with the technical documentation furnished; (c) the parts and materials used by licensee in the manufacture of products meet the requirements specified in the technical documentation furnished; (d) the resources and skills applied by licensee to the manufacture of the product are those of a manufacturer experienced in the manufacture of a product of similar complexity and manufacture; and (e) the design of the product conforms exactly to the design furnished by the licensor. (T. W. Hoya and D. D. Stein, "Drafting Contracts in US–Soviet Trade," *Law and Policy in International Business*, vol. 7 (1975), p. 1087.)

If you don't ask questions, even obvious ones, don't take umbrage when you realize later that you should have.

Take care to get included in the contract the right to revise all penalty dates once any one of them slips, because otherwise their negotiators will not agree to do so later and you are liable to be clobbered right through the life of the deal. Soviet officials seldom entertain variations in the terms of a contract once it has been agreed on, so either get it right from the start or don't sign it.

Performance negotiations with the Soviets can be harrow-, ing unless you regard these sessions as opportunities to concentrate entirely on your product's technical soundness and not as impertinent challenges to your company's reputation.

This is a dangerous time for you and under pressure, perhaps, to impress your opposite number with the high quality of your company's products, you may be trapped into claiming it can do more than you should. Aggressive sales patter sounds great at gung-ho presentations when an exaggerated claim ("this machine is so good it can make widgets on half power and be run by monkeys") is taken for a joke and not put down as evidence for the prosecution, whose clients have hired monkeys and tried to work through power cuts! Hence, under pressure, do not overcommit yourself or oversell your wonderful product.

Everything takes time and sometimes even longer

The problems of Soviet performance negotiations are compounded by their on–off nature. The Soviet Union does not run its affairs to suit your timetables. The engineering inspectors from the state committee that you met last month do not rush back to their offices and immediately send a fully written-up report on their negotiations to their superiors. Neither does it occur to the next layer of specialists—perhaps from the region where the plant that is going to use your product is sited—to immediately jump on a train or plane and come and see you, just because you are twiddling your thumbs in the Hotel Ukraine in Moscow.

Bureaucrats, especially those in Communist countries, are subject to multifarious pressures from above and below their niche in the structure they work in, and it is most unlikely that your timetable features very high on their list of priorities (which generally includes keeping their heads down and keeping out of controversy, given the drab alternatives for them if they screw things up).

They will get around to you and your negotiations about as fast as the notoriously slow Soviet waiters get around their restaurants. Indeed, even Soviet waiters can seem like greased lightning compared to some of the Kafka-esque bureaucrats you have to deal with (unless, of course, you are a supplier of something somebody way up the structure happens to want badly, in which case they might stir themselves—but not a great deal). It has been said that the Russian language does not include a word with quite the precise sense of urgency implied by *mañana!*

There is little point in your sending letters and telexes during the negotiations asking them what is happening. You won't find out much this way, so save your postage and wait. It takes longer to get approval to send a letter (evidence!) to the West on what is going on—mainly because they are unlikely to know themselves—than it does to let the decision process grind on regardless. If you really need to do business with the Soviets very badly you have certainly chosen the wrong market in which to get quick results.

Price negotiations

Price negotiations with Communist bureaucrats have special features. Not the least is the capacity of the average Soviet official to drive a hard bargain. Two generations of Communism have not yet knocked out of Soviet citizens a basic instinct for trading.

You are not dealing with guys who trade their assets for beads and broken mirrors. They may not know the true accounting cost of any of their economy's products, having adopted an accounting system devised by Stalin, who had a management style unaccountable to anybody, but they sure know the age-old trading principle of offering a little for a lot.

Their capacity as traders, allied to their political prejudices against the filthy rich capitalists who are trying to rip them off, forces them to put pressure on Western quoted prices, no matter how low or profitless your opening prices may be to you. They do not believe you when you claim to put up trimmed prices in the negotiations; they will not accept your first price under any circumstances, so you had better build in a negotiating margin from the start and fight to hold it to the bitter end.

You have two possible strategies. Start with your list prices (a copy of which they require as part of their documentation—though you could have a special one printed for them with all your prices upped by an appropriate premium to give you negotiating room later) and hold the slide below them to as small a discount as possible. Alternatively, start openly with a premium (say, 15 percent) above your list prices on the grounds that trading with Communist economies is fraught with additional risks and expense to you.

The first strategy is in my view a poor one, only partly rescued by the deception of a separate Soviet price list. Of course, your Soviet official has dreamed up some plausible-sounding arguments to tempt you to adopt it. The most frequent is his claim that, since he represents a monopoly trading organization, you need only sell once to him, and this must keep your marketing costs down which should be reflected in lower prices.

Comparable marketing costs in capitalist economies have to include several selling operations with each individual customer and hence, the Soviet official is not misleading you, except in respect to the time it takes to complete a full cycle of negotiations with him—two years is not an infrequent investment of time (and expense) for comradely negotiations.

The second strategy is preferable and must appeal to the negotiator in you, otherwise you're reading the wrong book. You should bear in mind that exporting your products involves additional costs to you over and above those of getting your products to your factory gate.

Sending negotiators on trips abroad costs cash and so do funding staff time for negotiating with overseas clients, sending out samples, exhibiting at fairs, promoting and advertising, corresponding, telephoning and telexing to customers, waiting for on-site inspection reports and negotiating consequential action from same, meeting special packing requirements, shipping the products to the ports (FOB) or to the customer (CIF), allowing for returns or breakdowns and putting the problem right, perhaps with your own engineers sent out as troubleshooters, and managing a service organization for the overseas buyer.

There is no reason (other than your gullibility) why you should absolve the Soviet buyer of the additional costs that arise as a direct result of serving him or any other overseas customer. You are not gilding the lily by seeking to cover your real costs of doing business with his country; you are merely arranging to stay in business in your own!

You will help yourself achieve the latter by watching the commitment to a fixed price at the start of your negotiations. Months, maybe years, later, those fixed prices will look suicidal to your accountants, and that's before the contract is finally signed. By the time deliveries are completed your fixed prices will be positively kamikaze. You can avoid such disasters by quoting prices good for ninety days in your initial bid for the business, and allowing for them to be revised upwards in line with Western inflation rates for the duration of the contract.

Soviet negotiators do not know much about inflation. All prices in Communist economies are fixed by the state and

DOING BUSINESS WITH IVAN COSTS YOU

The Soviet system for conducting foreign trade starts in the interests of the Soviet state and not the financial health of those eager to trade with them.

In order to tempt you into cutting your prices they will try the "sell cheap, get famous" gambit. "Low prices on this first order will lead to additional business later," they will tell you. The truth is, it won't. Under no circumstances trim your prices for future Soviet trade. As soon as they get a low price they will expect, nay, demand, that prices remain low forever.

Communist negotiators know all about intimidation (their political system is based on it), and they will try some of the oldest buyer's gambits in the history of negotiating. Among these there is, of course, "Noah's Ark" (it's been around that long!): "We cannot do business with you because your prices are too high compared to the prices of your competitors, with whom we are at this moment about to sign a deal."

In some versions of Noah's Ark they actually shout loudly, bang the table, and even stage a walkout. Your best response? Unflappability. Why? *It's always a bluff.* If they did have lower prices from the competition they would have no reason to talk to you. If you cut your prices on the basis of this performance, you are going to regret it.

Remember: It costs more to do business with the Soviets because you have to invest considerable resources, including executive time, in setting up the deal, probably over several years; you might be faced with heavy penalty payments, which you can bet a ruble to a kopeck they will collect on; it will cost you more to get insurance coverage and financial aid for your transactions; they expect your prices to remain stable, irrespective of inflation; and if interest rates are involved on the credits you provide to them for their purchases, they have a fixed interest rate of 6 percent applied to all of their business, regardless of what it costs you in the United States to borrow money. Hence, pad, don't strip, your quoted prices and hang on to them tenaciously.

don't change unless the state wants them to (so, instead of inflation, they have shortages of goods and long lines for those goods they do have). Therefore, the negotiators will resist a price inflator clause in the contract. On the other hand, they want your goods, and it is better if your negotiating stance requires them to learn to adjust to the phenomenon of Western inflation rather than requiring you to adjust to their noninflationary accounting system by following a kamikaze fixed-price policy.

Another cost that you must consider is that of the agent, if you are using one. An agent's commission is usually a percentage (straight or sliding) of the gross sale value. This either comes out of your profits (oh dear!) or is treated as a selling cost and added to your prices as a markup (always a sound thing to do).

Barter deals

Soviet price negotiations can be complicated by the preference for barter-only or part-barter deals among Communist foreign trade organizations. Their incentive to try for counter-trade deals is quite simple. They don't have a lot of "hard" cash that is suitable for foreign trade; the paper money they do have (the ruble) is of such international value that nobody outside a funny farm is likely to want it for other than wallpaper. (It is also illegal to import or export rubles across a Soviet frontier—so beware!)

The demand for a barter deal is part of the negotiation on price. Having tied you up in prolonged negotiations that have switched your "I've-got-a-deal" euphoria on and off like a Las Vegas hotel sign and having driven hard against your dollar price, they will introduce the demand to pay some, or even all (if they have your measure), of the cost of your products in the form of goods from a list they provide you with, and they will try damn hard to keep the number of items on that list as small as possible.

Faced with this obstacle, and afraid to lose a deal in which you have already invested much time and trouble in keeping alive for two years, you are under a lot of pressure to carry on and accept this twist in your fate. They know this, which is why they save the move until the precise moment when the pressure of your past investment is at its greatest. Instead of getting 300,000 dollars in cash, you could be faced with a demand (complete with theatricals out of the Eisenstein School of Dramatic Art) that you take half of it in candle wax or Rubik's Cubes.

You may be lucky and get a bargain, though don't bet on it. If what they offer could be sold easily for hard currency they would have tried that before they offered it to you, unless this is one of those bureaucratic messes that they are sometimes famous for, in which case you might end up grinning like a clown from the Russian state circus when you sell their barter goods to a delighted American customer.

In some deals, particularly in the chemical processing industry, part-payment may be offered from the output of the plant that you are supplying. In some commodity markets this can be acceptable, provided you are sure of the quality of the output and that it is of a composition usable in United States or third-party markets, and that you pay attention in the negotiations to the add-on costs of getting it out of the Soviet Union to where you can store, part-process, or sell it. A million barrels of petroleum crude in Omsk is a different proposition from the same cargo delivered to a Texan refinery.

The Soviet negotiators could assert that they can only finance your deal if you take barter goods or help them arrange the sale of some goods to a third party for hard currency. Time, risk, and expense must enter your mind when this is proposed. But watch it, as their next move could indicate that the barter demand was a double bluff to get you to seek to avoid the expenses of barter by offering them a discount off the cash price you have quoted!

These Russians are *not*, repeat NOT, anybody's fools when it comes to negotiating ploys and gambits. If you stay off the vodka and watch carefully, they might teach you something about how to do business, and lead you to be grateful that they are not competing with us as capitalists.

**TIPS FOR TRAVELERS IN
SOVIET TERRITORIES**

When in conversation with Eastern European negotiators do not introduce the topic of the Soviet Union. You may or may not be talking to dedicated Russophiles, and whether or not they are dedicated Communists need have nothing to do with their attitude to the Russians.

Do not carry with you anything that can be remotely connected with politics, including recent issues of any U.S. newspaper. Take particular care to have no books, especially those written by Soviet dissidents or detractors, that might be regarded as critical of the "socialist achievements" of the East. You should also avoid carrying religious tracts, more than one copy of the Bible, and certainly anything about Israel.

Entrepreneurs among you must forgo opportunities to make private deals with nationals of these countries, particularly in respect to foreign currency, but also including American-style clothes and personal effects. There are severe punishments if you are caught (hence, the attractive rates you will be offered), and such deals should be avoided, politely but firmly, on all occasions.

The situation regarding bath plugs is improving (why there is a shortage is a mystery), but you should still travel prepared and take a golf ball with you. Some toilet facilities are primitive, especially the stand-and-squat variety. The staff in the hotels used by foreigners are immovable in their routines; the women at the end of each corridor watch all bedroom arrivals and departures and never sleep; and the slothful service in the state retail organization, GUM, suggests it should be renamed GLUM.

Taxi drivers, hotel porters, and waiters expect to be tipped, (but *not* frontier guards, policemen, or officials). Small inexpensive presents—a company pen, a miniature bottle of Scotch, a picture postcard of your plant, town, or a memorial, a bunch of flowers—are permissible as gifts. You will be inundated with tin badges, flowers, and notepads. You may be surprised at how many ordinary people speak English.

If offered a sexual encounter, resist the temptation. It is not unknown for foreigners to be blackmailed for their company's secrets.

Be moderate in your drinking too. Formal lunches can involve several toasts (to mutual friendship between your countries, to world peace, to the women of the world, to the children of the world, to peaceful coexistence, to the dead of the Great Patriotic War, to the president of the USSR and the president of the United States, to International Knitting Machinists' Day, and so on), and you are expected to swallow the, usually neat, vodka in one go, ready for another for the next toast. Get smart and keep your glass filled with mineral water or lemonade, which is always provided on the table.

Appointments with Communist officials and negotiators should be kept punctually. They do not like to be kept waiting. Appointments can take some time to arrange. So can visas. It is said that the real reason why Soviet spy Kim Philby hung around Beirut while waiting to flee to Moscow was that it took that long for his visa to come through!

There is little in the way of American entertainment, but most Communist countries have excellent museums and historic buildings to visit, and well worth it they are too. You will not find much in the world to beat Leningrad's Hermitage. There is a strong emphasis everywhere on official state politics—posters, statues, banners, and billboards show endless effigies of Marx, Engels, and Lenin and countless slogans. The Great Patriotic War (World War II) is remembered everywhere. Keep out of trouble by showing respect—remember what you are there for.

ANSWERS TO SELF-ASSESSMENT TEST 3

1 **a** Not likely to be a problem at a preliminary meeting. They will concentrate on technical specifications first. However, if you are price-conscious you will always invite a price objection.   (−5)

b Yes. They will go over your technical specifications with great care, so be ready for this.   (10)

c Not a question at first. However, although the Soviet economic system is not very efficient, once you commit yourself to a delivery date you had better keep it or you will face a penalty charge.   (−5)

d Soviet negotiators take a great (even obsessive) interest in performance standards, but you should know what your products can do and hence this ought not to be a problem.   (−7)

e Export licenses can prove to be a big problem, given the prohibition in the United States regarding exporting products that can have military applications. Make sure that your deal is conditional on your getting a U.S. export license.   (3)

f Could be a problem at the end of the negotiation and will require both firmness and imagination on your part. Pad your prices beforehand, otherwise you might end up with a loss.   (5)

2 **a** It is almost impossible to develop a personal relationship with a Soviet negotiator and not very wise anyway.   (−10)

b By far the best policy. Show respect but do not get too involved.
(10)

3 **a** Soviet negotiators often try to intimidate you into dropping your price because of alleged competition. Resist this ploy. If you are a price-crumbler you should stay at home.   **(−10)**

b You are a price-crumbler!   **(−10)**

c No! That is why they try to pressure you with the alleged competition.   **(−10)**

d Yes! Alleged competition is *never* a reason for moving on your prices.   **(10)**

SELF-ASSESSMENT TEST 4

1 You are in Kobe, Japan, discussing the possibility of business with a local company, and the leader of the Japanese team hands you a colorfully wrapped box which is clearly intended as a personal gift. Do you:

a Thank him profusely and open the box?
b Thank him profusely and put the box away?
c Thank him profusely and hand him a gift in return?

2 On arrival at Narita airport, Tokyo, you are met by your Japanese hosts, who kindly inquire as to your return journey, offering to check your reservations for you and to handle any related matters during your stay. Do you regard this as:

a An example of Japanese courtesy?
b A means of finding out your deadlines?

3 When you are considering doing business with a Japanese company, which of the following would you and they consider to be the most important?

a The profitability of your company
b Its market share
c Its growth rate
d Its labor relations

CHAPTER 4

The Land of the Rising Yen—or, Where Not to Take Yes for an Answer

Change and continuity

Japan is different. It is also rapidly growing into the world's largest national economy. At present it is the second largest industrial power. The United States is the largest and will remain so for much of the rest of the twentieth century, but beyond that it is likely that Japan will become number one.

Unlike in the United States, which relies on international trade for only 10 percent of its multitrillion-dollar economy, in Japan the proportion is more like 20 percent. That means it is, and will remain, in the business of trading worldwide for its living. This also means that it is more than likely that your own business interests are going to be influenced, directly or indirectly, by the Japanese. Either you will buy from or sell to them, in which case you had better get your act together as a negotiator, or you will buy or sell in competition with them, in which case you had better get your act even more together!

The Japanese are unique because of the way they have handled the transition from a traditional and ancient society to a bustling and modern one. In many ways they are a model for those who also wish to combine change with maintaining traditional values and mores more or less as they have been for centuries. Much of the unrest faced by the late Shah of Iran was caused by the clash between tradition and change (the old way versus modernization), and it is said that if there is ever going to be real trouble in Saudi Arabia it will arise from the conflict of the values of purist Islam with the sins of progress.

Japan's process of change began with the Meiji restoration in 1868, and by excelling in modernization without overturning its traditional values the process has continued until the country is on the brink of overtaking the United States economically.

The role of courtesy

To do business with the Japanese you must make some effort to understand how they function. Better still, if you have the time, you should try to appreciate *why* they function the way they do. The shortest way to express what I mean here is to say that for the Japanese everything is managed by a strict code of courtesy.

Courtesy is more than just being polite. In a traditional society courtesy expresses the role everybody has in the "proper" (that is, traditional) order of things. When people interact within their own group, their manners express mutual recognition of their membership in the group. When people interact with people in other groups, courtesy enables them to interact in mutual recognition of each other's group role.

Hence, members of a family behave in a certain way with each other, and they behave in a certain way with members of other families. Courtesy facilitates contact between individuals in a way that does not threaten the established order, whether this is the family, the company, the government, or whatever.

As an American, you will have extended to you the courtesies of the group or groups to which you are properly introduced and admitted. From the moment that you hand over your own business card and find it studied by your Japanese contact—who will have handed his over with the same expectation—you will be drawn into a social system without parallel in the United States.

How rapidly you build up your rapport with your Japanese opposite number will determine whether and to what extent you will do business. You cannot overestimate the role of mutual respect, friendliness, and rapport in your relations with the Japanese.

CARDS PLEASE!

The exchange of business cards in Japan is an absolutely essential ritual, so you must go prepared with several hundred cards, preferably printed on one side in English and on the other in Japanese.

Do not underestimate the social requirement for exchanging your card with *everybody* that you meet. This includes offering and receiving one card for every person in the room, even if there are twenty people at the meeting on both sides!

An American negotiator once exchanged 112 business cards at the start of a session. It took fifteen minutes to complete the ritual, and he knew that there was no way honor and mutual respect could be satisfied until he had been around the entire room to each person to exchange a bow and a card. He also made sure that he looked carefully at the cards he was offered, even though many of them were in Japanese without English translations.

Much of what passes for quaint custom and ritual in Japan is actually an expression of their need to check you and your company (and its propositions) for signs that there is potential for long and fruitful business based on strong and enduring personal relationships.

If you are in a hurry, or do not consider personal relationships of any value, or cannot abide messing about with highly polite (to most Americans, almost excessively polite) exchanges of conversation, gifts, and kindnesses; or if you are, to the Japanese mind, quite rude, you are unlikely to secure much interest in what you have come to sell or buy.

Japanese use of time

The role of time in negotiating with the Japanese can easily be misunderstood. I certainly misunderstood it for some years, until I became more familiar with the Japanese mode of business. For example, in *Everything Is Negotiable!* (1983) I drew attention to the potential weakness that a deadline can create for an American negotiator. I did this by asking a self-assessment question similar to question 2 at the beginning of this chapter. The question derives from the experience of negotiators who on their arrival in Japan are met by their contacts and go through the ritual of having their air reservations scrutinized. Ostensibly, I suggested, this was done in the interests of extending a service but really had another, hidden, motivation. I implied in my earlier book that the real purpose behind this move was for the Japanese to discover the deadline toward which an American negotiator would be working, in order to use this information to apply pressure and secure concessions.

The truth is slightly more complicated (though with some Japanese my original implication may have some foundation). Time is needed by the Japanese to consider all the implications of a business proposal, and they carry out the necessary consultation much more thoroughly than is common in the United States.

The Japanese process of consultation (*ringi-seido*) could bring to the surface problems not appreciated or known to the senior managers negotiating on behalf of the company. This event in turn will require further consultations to see what can be done to remove the problems. All of this takes time as the decision passes up and down the company structure.

Meanwhile the U.S. negotiator will be kept waiting. Nothing he does can hurry up the process, although impatient intervention during it or signs of disapproval could slow it down or even make it unnecessary—they could decide that you are showing disrespect and are not the sort of person with whom they want to do any business.

In part, my earlier view was based on discussions with other negotiators to whom the airport incident had happened, from which they derived the conclusions alluded to in my answer to the self-assessment question. From additional experience I now see that these conclusions were in error, or at least not the complete picture.

Let me explain. There is no doubt that American negotiators operate at a different pace from their Japanese counterparts. This reflects the different decision-making systems common to well-managed companies in each culture. The Japanese take what seems to be an inordinate amount of time to reach a decision. This is because their management system requires that a full consultation take place with all persons in the organization who are likely to be influenced by the decision.

This approach contrasts with the normal American one of sales staff who often make commitments on behalf of their company which are not necessarily confirmed beforehand by their production counterparts. As we all know, sales person-

SUMO WRESTLING AND NEGOTIATING

The Japanese can spend what appears to Westerners to be an unprecedented amount of time in preliminaries before discussing their business. These preliminaries have, however, an essential role to play and cannot be skipped if you want to get the best deal that is available.

An international banker, with many years' experience in negotiating with the Japanese on joint U.S.–Japanese ventures, explained it in the following way:

Negotiating with the Japanese goes through several phases, of which the first is probably the most crucial (the other phases, in the main, follow internationally recognized norms).

The opening phase is like two Sumo wrestlers facing each other before the start of their contest. They make highly ritualized and absolutely expected genuflections, and go through a detailed ritual involving salt being thrown in each corner and much bowing and other demonstrations of respect.

Then they engage each other's attention and prepare themselves. They examine each other and pace their breathing, gradually increasing the tempo until they are both sure that they are ready. Then, and only then, do they lunge forward.

Neither will move toward the other until absolutely sure that they are in balance with each other, both physically and mentally.

It is the need to get into mutual balance that distinguishes Japanese businessmen in their contacts with non-Japanese negotiators. Only when they feel on the same wavelength will they begin their business, and all that precedes this stage is aimed at achieving interpersonal harmony.

JADE POT BLAMES RED KETTLE

A Japanese negotiating team met their match when they spent many fruitless months trying to negotiate a business deal with the Soviet Union. The Japanese specialized in heavy machinery for surface mineral extraction, and the Soviet government wanted to acquire their technology for use in Siberia.

The negotiating teams from the two cultures did not get on at all well. In fact, negotiations got bogged down, and the Japanese returned home more than a little demoralized from their experiences. Their complaints make an interesting comment on aspects of Japanese methods of doing business and should be studied by those trying to understand their outlook.

First, the Japanese complained that their opposite numbers on the Soviet team were quite uninterested in developing personal relationships and rebuffed all Japanese attempts at conviviality. Moreover, the Soviet team changed personnel several times during the six months the Japanese were in Prestoplavsk.

Second, they claimed the Soviets took an excessively long time to make a decision. This will cause a wry smile among those who negotiate with Japanese companies and indicate just how long the Soviets must have been taking if it was so long that the Japanese felt they had cause to complain about it!

Third, the Japanese felt that the Soviets, because of their monopoly position as the sole customer for Japanese products in Siberia, were using unfair tactics by having several Japanese companies competing for the same business and by keeping them apart from each other in case they might compare notes.

Fourth, the Japanese were appalled at the amount of detail the Soviet negotiators wanted (implying to them that the Japanese were not capable of producing world-class machinery), and they were apprehensive at the extent of the proposed contract that the Soviets wanted them to sign (implying a lack of trust in Japanese commitments).

Last, the Japanese complained that Prestoplavsk was an awful place to spend much time in and that their Soviet hosts left them to their own devices for social entertainment, often for days on end. Also, they only got decisions to go ahead on important details just as they had to leave to get transport home.

nel can and do promise potential clients almost anything to get the order, including performance levels, quantities, and delivery dates that are not possible in practice. This causes the familiar tension between sales and production (and between sales and accounting—the former preferring that the company hold vast inventories of everything just in case a customer wants to buy one, and the latter preferring that the company have no inventories at all because they tie up capital).

A well-managed Japanese company (although not all Japanese companies are well managed) will require that a commitment offered to another company be endorsed by those whose actions will determine in practice if that commitment is to be met.

Failure to meet a commitment is a serious matter, and the Japanese prefer to take time before they make a commitment to make sure that everybody (and I mean *everybody*) in the organization understands the commitment and agrees to its being given. They don't want to be forced to spend time later trying to sort out what to do about a commitment that should not have been given in the first place and to have to chastise those who have failed in some way to honor the commitment given in the company's name.

If a delivery date is being given, then clearly those parts of the company responsible for designing, constructing, and completing the product will have to be consulted to see if they can meet that date. A Japanese company requires a formal written endorsement from each manager responsible for each activity and will expect him to have consulted his workforce before he gives his endorsement.

When an American company overextends itself this creates problems for those whose job is made more difficult as a consequence. The usual message from the top of an American company that has overextended itself to those who feel overwhelmed as a result of this situation is often a four-letter word: Cope! A Japanese company avoids this by in-depth consultation and agreement beforehand.

American perceptions of deadlines

From the point of view of an uninformed negotiator who makes a short visit to Japan in order to sign an agreement, the details of which he plans to negotiate face-to-face with his Japanese contacts, the reasons for delays in getting a decision look quite different from those described above. We always assume the worst when we contemplate the source of our inconvenience.

You assume that the delay is aimed at putting on negotiating pressure as your deadline to return home approaches. "Didn't they make a point of inquiring when I had to leave?" "Isn't it the case that we've spent several weeks in socializing, with short bursts of negotiating activity lasting a day or so and now, just as I have two days left before departing, they're presenting me with amended proposals?"

The answers convince you that you are dealing with tactics aimed at using your deadlines to pressure you into making concessions. When you add to your suspicions the fact that you did make concessions in those last hurried meetings before walking onto your departing aircraft, you complete your

WHO'S BOTHERED ABOUT PENALTIES?

A Hong Kong shipping company needed to replace some of its bulk carriers and opened negotiations with a Japanese yard before placing their order. They were used to negotiations with European shipbuilders taking the normal route of hard bargaining on prices and just as hard bargaining on the size of the penalty payments for (the expected) late delivery. They felt they had gotten a good deal when shipbuilders offered a four million dollar penalty for late delivery.

The Japanese matched European prices for building the ships and promised as good a delivery date. When it came to the penalty price for late delivery, however, the Japanese invited the Hong Kong managers to write into the contract "any sum you like; we will not argue over the amount." This caught the Hong Kong negotiators by surprise, and they asked if the Japanese were serious, expecting a long argument about delivery penalties.

"Of course we are serious," the Japanese insisted. "Fill in the total price of the ship if you like."

This told the Chinese, beyond any doubt, that the Japanese were certain to meet their delivery promises. This was in contrast to the long haggles they had experienced with other shipbuilders.

The order went to the Japanese yard.

belief that deadline hustling is a peculiarly Japanese tactic.

It might look that way, but it almost certainly is not (though no one can blame the Japanese if they accept the concessions offered to them by a time-pressured American negotiator). Delays during a negotiation are a consequence of a necessary part of their management system. The amended proposals they present to you on their return to the negotiations will have arisen out of their consultations and will represent the consensus of their management team. The fact that you are now in a hurry to return to whence you came is not their fault; their earlier interest in your departure deadline was purely one of ascertaining what time they had available for doing business with you.

The counter to deadline pressure, from whatever source you experience it, is, of course, not to have deadlines in the first place. If you go to Japan to do business in a hurry it is your sense of time that is wrong, not theirs. If you went to Japan with the intention of spending a month or more, thus giving them time to consult their people, you would not be under the self-inflicted pressure of your own deadlines. There is nothing to stop you taking a longer time to conduct your business with the Japanese. (If there is, perhaps you should try selling to Brazil rather than to Japan.) You can just as easily visit them and then leave your proposals on the table while they think about them and arrange to get their own management's agreement. You can always use the time available to visit other companies or other parts of the same company, or you can return in a month or two when they are ready to reply with their considered response.

If you insist on everything being settled in a week or ten days, you are going to be as disappointed as you are suspicious. Hence, the time pressure that many American negotiators feel they are the victims of is often the result of their own attempt to pressure the Japanese into an earlier settlement than they are ready for. Think of your behavior from their point of view: Why is this person in such a hurry? Is there something in his proposals that we have not noticed? Perhaps we should reexamine them.

International negotiators have to accept that the pace of a negotiation will always be determined by the pace of the dominant party. If this is clearly understood by the negotiator visiting Japan, it will produce a lot of respect from the Japanese, and in Japan business goes to those whom the other party respects the most.

The quest for technical details

Like the Soviets, the Japanese are avaricious when it comes to acquiring technical details of your products, though the motivation in the Japanese case is somewhat more honorable. The Soviet negotiator seeks to protect himself from accepting something that is not quite kosher and at the same time engages in some *en passant* technological espionage. The Japanese are more likely to be establishing through their technical queries the technical soundness of the product and your own suitability as a person in whom to entrust their business future.

If they are going to acquire a license to manufacture your product, they must, of course, know everything there is to know about it. Likewise, if they are going to act as agents in Japan to sell your product, at the very least their own sales agents and service people will need to know everything they can.

The meetings that take place between your team and theirs in Japan will involve considerable amounts of time spent interrogating (there is no other word for it) you and your team, and not just on the technical qualities of what you produce. They will expect you to know the finest details of the financial arrangements of your business, including market share, growth rates, and the intricacies of your company's place in the wider context of the industry you are in; and, where applicable, about your company's structure if you are a subsidiary of a larger organization.

Profits or growth?

American business negotiators tend to be more concerned with profitability than with growth rates, which is opposite to the Japanese. The difference is interesting, though its basis is not entirely a cultural one. It reflects the entrepreneurial psychology more common in expanding Japan than in the more recession-obsessed West. Several U.S. entrepreneurs are more Japanese in their attitudes to growth than their contemporaries, which verifies that this difference in outlook is not entirely culture-based.

The Japanese business leader will study the relative market shares of his own and rival companies in all of the product lines he handles. He will be interested in growth rates of sales and the steady drive to dominate in each sector of the market. His judgments about how well a company is managed will be influenced greatly by what he sees in these figures.

Whether a plant is profitable or, more correctly (because some level of profit is required if a business is to be sustained), how profitable the business is will be of less interest to him. Indeed, exceptionally high (by Japanese standards) profit levels could actually cause him to worry, for this indicates to him that something is wrong with the sales drive.

The Japanese will always opt for increasing their outlays on sales (both by direct marketing and by aggressive prices) rather than for accumulating high profits. They live their business lives on the edge of constant growth instead of in safe consolidation of previously successful products. The entrepreneurial American businessman behaves in much the same fashion, with the difference that he is more likely to be an exception in his own country, rather than, as in Japan, the rule.

Attitudes to investment

A few very large companies dominate the domestic Japanese market. They also dominate import business. They rely heavily on bank-financed loans for their operations and their expansion. They do not worry too much about the ratio of debt interest to profits as long as they are expanding, and to expand they must invest in extending their capacity to produce more.

The contrast with an American business is stark. A U.S. corporation will see investment as a means of reducing labor while maintaining output. This leads to lower unit costs and therefore, at least in theory, to increased or maintained unit profits while the corporation does much as it did the previous year.

A Japanese company will see investment in equipment as a means of expanding output with the same workforce and regard the job of selling the additional output as a challenge to its philosophy of growth. Nowhere is the consequence of this different approach seen more clearly than in the attitude of their labor force to the role of investment. In the United States, new technology is equated with job losses and therefore resisted; in Japan new technology is equated with preserving employment and therefore accepted.

These differences in outlook explain some of the differences in the preparation negotiators in each country will undertake prior to meeting to discuss potential business opportunities. The U.S. corporation will study the Japanese firm's financial soundness and its profitability (assuming it studies anything at all). The Japanese firm will study the U.S. corporation's relative position in its markets, its suppliers, its customers, and its organizational connections (if relevant) with associated companies in the holding group. In early meetings the Japanese will expect the American negotiators to know in minute detail everything about their corporation's financial structure and the financial structure of all corporations, including rivals, suppliers, and customers, with which they compete or deal.

When it comes to price negotiations the Japanese will tend toward aggressive price policies that will maximize sales, not profits. To get into a market they will expect to take losses and will not worry too much about so doing. This puts a lot of pressure on American corporations that follow a different pricing policy, assuming that they want to do business with or in Japan.

Avoid contract jargon

Another area where there might be a difference in approach, and because of this danger to good relations and harmony, is in the question of contracts between the parties. The Japanese are at the other end of the spectrum in the matter of contracts from the Soviets, who normally require the most detailed specification of mutual obligations, including penalty clauses, incorporated into the contract before agreement is reached. With the Japanese the exact opposite tends to be the case.

Business relations for the Japanese are not separated from the mutual respect each party has for the other. In fact, they are an integral part of the same experience. A tightly drawn-up contract in the usual legal language common to U.S. business practice ("party of the first part," "party of the second part" and so on) is anathema to the Japanese approach.

First, English legal language is mind-boggling even to the English-speaking, and, one suspects, few U.S. lawyers fully understand it themselves. (They certainly charge enough for giving conflicting interpretations of the same document!) This presents an enormous problem when the terms are translated into Japanese. It's bad enough trying to translate a U.S. contract into plain English.

Second, the implication of a heavily documented legal contract written in formal legal language is that the parties need to cover themselves for every eventuality. Now, some eventualities are of a sensitive nature (what happens if they run off with the loot?), and if these are presented in a stark way to a Japanese negotiator at the start of what is intended to be a mutually beneficial relationship, you run the risk of causing great offense. If you feel you need to cover yourself against the prospect of their being dishonest, or of their failing to meet their obligations in some way, they are likely to think that you do not trust or respect them.

In short, they prefer not to do business with people who do not treat them with respect. What might be taken for granted in Europe—the need to avoid "one-truck contracts" (that is, contracts that leave both parties at the mercies of Murphy's Law)—if handled carelessly can be deeply offensive in Japan.

This is not an unsurmountable problem. My advice is to keep your legal people at arm's length and to require of them that they explain in straightforward English what their legal mumbo jumbo means, in language that can be translated into Japanese with the least chance of causing misunderstanding. Better still, work from a Japanese contract and add in only what is absolutely necessary.

Japanese corporations do not engage in deliberate malpractices, nor do they cheat those with whom they share their business. You can relax a little more than you normally would.

Nothing I have said here should be interpreted as suggesting that the Japanese do not participate in negotiating a contract. They do, and they will insist on being very specific in terms of quality, performance, quantity, delivery, and specifications. They will also hold to the terms of the contract, but what they find difficult to accept is a multiclause contract drawn up in legalistic language. This suggests from the start that their intentions are suspect or that the worst must be prepared for or insured against.

Importance of personal relationships

The Japanese hold very strongly to the importance of personal relationships in their business dealings. They like to get to know the people with whom they intend to do business, and they like to deal with the same people over and over again. Here they are not unlike the Chinese, who reserve a special place in their negotiations for "old friends"—foreigners they have dealt with before or who are introduced to them by somebody they revere or trust, usually another "old friend." Negotiators in South America are similar. They too like to "relate" to the people who want to do business with them. If this proves not possible—the chemistry is wrong, for example—it is unlikely that business will be contracted.

The domination of interpersonal relations in the outlook and approach of Japanese negotiators finds its popular expression in the almost total inability of the Japanese to utter the word "no," even when they wish to do so, and their substitution of a complicated, though unintentional, prevarication when put into a situation where to an American "no" would be the appropriate answer.

Being almost unable to say no, they can be misunderstood when they say yes (*hai!*). If you have asked a question that requires them to say no, it is your fault for asking the question in that way should you end up disappointed by their inability to deliver on the yes. (A similar problem is found among the Arabs. Saying no implies that they do not *want* to help, so they say yes even if they have no means of fulfilling that commitment.)

This can be very off-putting when you hear a stream of "Hai! Hai!" sounds and think he is saying yes to your proposals. He might just be letting you know that he is listening to what you have to say. This trait leads to the indirect approach in conversation. To tell you that your proposition is unacceptable by saying no would give offense, so he will say words to the effect that your proposal "could be better if it took in this or that." How many *this*'s or *that*'s will tell you just how unacceptable your proposition is!

Listening for signals from a Japanese negotiator is even more essential than when you are dealing with your own colleagues. The Japanese will try to nudge you toward what they want rather than go at you with a direct proposition, particularly if it contradicts something for which you have expressed a preference or where it could indicate that they have not been paying attention. Hence, avoid asking them if they have understood your proposition, as they will say "Hai!" even if you were totally incomprehensible.

In the land of the rising yen (and it will continue to rise for many a year yet) it is best if you are exceptionally polite and completely relaxed about time, and remember that you must never take yes for an answer!

ANSWERS TO SELF-ASSESSMENT TEST 4

1　a Always thank your Japanese hosts for anything they do for you, even well beyond the point at which your thanks would be cause for comment in the United States. But do not open any wrapped gift in these circumstances, unless expressly urged to do so by the person who gave it to you. There is a danger that he or she might lose face by offering to you a gift that is too expensive (compared to the one you intended to give) or too cheap. (−5)

　b Yes. In putting it away do so carefully, and tell the person who gave it to you how unworthy you are to receive such generous treatment. (5)

　c Even better. A small gift, neatly wrapped in traditional Japanese-design paper and tied with a nice bow, is always welcome. The value is less important than the thought. If you were unprepared for the gift exchange ritual, do not panic. A small token at the time, followed by a proper gift at the next opportunity, will do fine. In this respect, if your Japanese partner requires something that you promise to send on to him, *do so,* even at the cost of extraordinary effort. It will pay you back many times over.   (10)

2 a It is more than likely. The Japanese are exceptionally polite and go out of their way to help you. It is best to treat this event with an open mind (and, just to make sure that it is a courtesy only, always travel to Japan with open return tickets without a deadline on them).   (5)
   b They could have this motivation, though much of the problem with American negotiators is their tendency to try to rush things in Japan. The deadlines that they feel strangled by are often of their own making.   (−5)

3 a This is unlikely to be a decisive consideration.   (−5)
   b Yes. Your market share tells them about your market strengths or weaknesses. If you are seeking to supply their markets they will expect large volume from you; if you are seeking to represent them in your territory they will want you to do so only if you can move large volumes for them.   (10)
   c A high growth rate can compensate for a currently low market share. It will also tell them how entrepreneurial you and your company are and what they can expect from you.   (5)
   d Japanese industrial relations can be stormy. Their interest in your industrial relations would reflect their estimate of your capacity to produce output or provide a service. In Japanese eyes constant strikes over trivial issues suggest that there is something wrong with your management.   (3)

SELF-ASSESSMENT TEST 5

1 You are arranging to visit a number of Arab countries to promote your products and to secure local agencies to distribute them in local markets. How many days do you allow for your itinerary, which is to include Egypt, Saudi Arabia, Oman, Kuwait, Iraq, and Libya?

a Seven
b Fourteen
c Eighteen
d Twenty-one
e Twenty-eight
f Thirty-one

2 You have been given an interview with a leading local Arab agent and have spent several hours socializing and drinking coffee. No business has been talked about and you are anxious to get the discussion of your proposals under way. Do you:

a Raise the subject in a lull in the conversation?
b Wait until your host raises the matter?

3 You have decided to wait until your host raises the subject, and now it is time for you to leave. Do you:

a Ask him when you can return to see him?
b Leave a set of materials about your products?
c Ask him for a definite date for an interview to discuss your business?

CHAPTER 5

Negotiating with the Arabs—or, How to Take Your Time

The Islamic family

Whereas with the Communists the state is the dominating influence in their business lives, with the Arabs it is the extended family (father, brothers, uncles, in-laws, and cousins). Obligations to one's family and friends are not treated lightly; they create, and are created by, mutual expectations of help, assistance, support, and succor. Warm-hearted nepotism rules or at least holds sway.

Your problem as a foreign negotiator can be summed up simply: You are not related to any Arab family, and therefore you are an outsider, a true foreigner in their land. If you compound your lack of familial ties by being ignorant of Arab customs, manners, and outlooks (or, worse, disrespectful of them) you will find it very difficult to make much headway in your business relationships with Arabs.

The Arab nation consists of 160 million people in twenty-two states spread across Northern Africa and the Middle East from the Atlantic Ocean to the Gulf of Oman. While there are vast variations in outlook, practice, and economic capacity among the Arab states, there are certain unifying forces in their societies that keep the spirit of Arab unity alive and which occasionally blow a little life into its practical application.

The Arabic language is among the most prominent of the unifying forces in the region. Dialects and accents there may be, but the written language and its classical roots reign supreme from one end of the Arab nation to the other. Those who would hope to do a lot of business with Arabs would do well to learn their language, if only to a rudimentary level. In the meantime, many Arab businessmen speak English (and sometimes French) and have degrees and diplomas from Western universities.

The other main unifying force is Islam, for though Islam is now a religious way of life for many beyond the Arab nation, it remains for the majority of Arabs a living memory of their history. It pervades all their social structures, and in many of their states it has a grip on the secular life that recognizes no separation of church and state.

Some countries, such as Saudi Arabia, Sudan, or Libya, are more Islamic in their secular laws than others, such as Egypt or Bahrain, though the differences are often more of degree than kind. The availability of or punishment for having booze is a reliable, if crude, guide to the Islamic temperature of a country.

While it is not necessary to convert to Islam to do business, it is sensible to learn something about Islam, its history, and its creeds and to treat its modern manifestations with respect. You must not mock by word or grimace anything you find unusual in the Arabs' behavior, and you must make no derogatory or joking remarks about their beliefs and customs, especially since much of what passes for knowledge of Islam in America is grotesquely inaccurate.

If it is Ramadan, your Arab host will not be eating or drinking until sunset and no matter how hungry or thirsty you are, you should try to avoid both food and tea, unless your host has it brought for you into his *diwan* (a room for receiving guests) and to refuse might give offense. But even then, acknowledge that you know it is Ramadan for him, and nibble or sip unenthusiastically at it rather than wolf it down as though it were your last supper.

If you are insensitive to this type of situation it might very well *be* your last supper as far as business with him is concerned, in which case you will eat, drink, and go home empty-handed.

The open door policy

Negotiations with Arabs can never be divorced from their environment, and it is for this environment that you must be prepared. By environment, I don't just mean that sand will be blown into your every orifice (though that is a distinct possibility upcountry), or that it gets very hot during the day and perishing cold at night. The environment I refer to has more to do with the social environment that influences Arab behavior as negotiators.

Take their "open door" policy, for instance. You may well be deep into discussion with an Arab contractor when some of his friends or family arrive at his office. They will certainly not be kept waiting outside the room but will be invited in for tea and talk. Your negotiations will be suspended until they leave, and they will continue only for as long as it takes for some more of his friends to arrive. And so it could go on all during your visit to his office, although there are some signs that the use of the traditional open door policy is being curbed by the more commercially minded of the Arabs.

The Arab will not refuse traditional hospitality to those who come to see him, and he can be diverted for many hours a day by social interruptions. You must accept this, no matter how important you might feel you are or how crucial your timetable is to you. It is not rudeness on his part. Quite the contrary, it is simply the continuation of the courtesies of the bedouin desert tradition, every bit as necessary for his functioning as a respected person in his society as it is for you to turn up at work in your suit and not your pajamas.

This open door habit infuriates some American negotiators. If you show signs of impatience to your host, you will be finished. I know one Harvard Law graduate who swore to me that he would never return to Egypt, no matter what the fee. He could not stand having his work day prolonged by the constant interruptions in his discussions with Arab civil servants, for whom the open door policy operates within government departments for absolutely anybody, their lowest clerks included—even though they (or rather their fathers and grandfathers) long ago left the imperatives of desert hospitality behind them.

In one respect I had to concur with his draconian decision. If you can't accept Arab ways, don't waste your time trying to do business with them.

The Arab attitude to time

The Arab attitude to time can give an entirely wrong impression to those brought up closer to the clock than is probably good for them. Americans are often obsessed with time, while Arabs can appear to be totally devoid of any consciousness of it.

Many Arabs know that time is more important than they or their colleagues acknowledge by their behavior, and attitudes are gradually changing. No doubt a compromise somewhere between the two extremes would do everybody a little good, but the low value placed on time has environmental roots which cannot be ignored just because it is inconvenient to our attitudes.

The Arabs are not the only nation to place a low value on

time. The Italians, Spanish, Portuguese, and Mexicans, among others, are notorious for adherence to the *mañana, mañana* school of decision making. It reflects the nonurban life-style of a preindustrial society, and it withers only as fast as the effects of urbanization and industrialization spread through the generations.

Hoping for quick decisions from Arabs can be a frustrating experience. On the other hand, they can make quick decisions on occasion (and deciding not to trust you could be one of them).

Their taking a long time to come to a decision about a proposition may not just be an example of muddling and inefficiency, though this can be the explanation in some cases. It might indicate that they are displeased with something in your proposition and that, though they have hinted at what is displeasing them, you have not picked up their signals and have not responded to them positively.

If you feel harassed by what you regard as time wasting, you certainly will not hear or note the signals. If you slow down to their pace of doing business, however, and listen carefully to what they are saying, you will learn to spot a problem and react by amending your proposition in the same way. (Much the same advice applies to negotiating with the Japanese.)

Subtle signals

In a sense, a negotiation with an Arab is partly a consultation with him. If you are doing well in your negotiations, you will hear yourself saying, "Here is what I was thinking of suggesting. What do you think of it?" far more than you will confront him with, "That's my final offer, take it or leave it."

If you do not reformulate aspects of an unsatisfactory proposition you have put to them, rather than say no to your face they will not make a decision at all. They hope time will allow them to get their way or will permit the issue to die naturally by neglect.

As you brood over your dilemma ("Why are they avoiding me?") you might, just might, go over what they said about your proposition and identify, by luck or by judgment, what the problem is. In representing the issue, assuming you have got it right this time, you might be surprised by the sudden change in pace as you both move on toward agreement.

If you don't see the problem at all, you will return home cursing the inefficiency of a nation "that was still riding around on camels while we were in high school" (as my Harvard friend somewhat impudently put it).

Arabs do not like face-to-face confrontations or quarrels with foreigners. They have a tradition of hospitality and politeness. The door that is open to the cousin or the neighbor is also open to you. You have come a long way to see them, and they respect that. They will go out of their way to make you welcome, no matter what other urgent business is at hand. Providing you do not upset them with your arrogance and haughtiness (the two qualities Arab negotiators identify in Americans as the ones they find most unacceptable), you will eventually get around to talking about business.

They do not like rushing into business subjects as soon as they meet with you. It is bad manners to do so, and they will expect you to talk with them about social and other matters for some time—perhaps fifteen minutes or more on most occasions, though sometimes for several hours or, on special occasions, through several meetings.

Your best plan is to leave to the Arab negotiator the decision of when to talk business. Do not under any circumstances be the first to raise the subject.

This can be very off-putting, especially when you have met the Arab for the first time and as far as you know, he does not know why you have come to see him. In your mind is the thought that unless you tell him that you are looking for a local agent to market your binoculars and range finders, he might think that you are a tourist just passing through the Gulf on your way to play polo in Delhi. Again, if you are tempted to raise the matter of business first, in one word—don't!

If the interview is clearly at an end, very politely thank him for his generous hospitality, and ask if you can come and see him on another day. He will certainly not refuse to see you again (here the open door works for you!), and you can try anew.

The Arab businessman may behave generously to a fault and sometimes appears to have an otherworldly naiveté about him, but he is not at all as stupid as the ignorant might think. Indeed, there are more Arab graduates of Western universities sitting across the carpet negotiating with American businessmen than there are American graduates sitting across the carpet negotiating with Arabs!

If you show that you understand the social mores of the Arab peoples your host will be more likely to talk business with you when you meet again. If, however, he is away when you next return to see him or is in and meets with you but does not discuss business, it suggests either that you must keep trying on another occasion or that he is telling you, without being rude, that he does not want to be an agent for binoculars and range finders. (He will have found out why you are in Doha or Bahrain without your knowing about it.)

Another word of caution is due here. If he does ask you why you have come to see him, do not start off with a sales pitch along the lines of "I am about to offer you a great opportunity to get rich as an agent for my company's products," which is an OK line in Gary, Indiana, but totally out of place in the Middle East.

It is far better to make your pitch along the lines of your wanting his help in a business proposition. He is unlikely to need to get richer and will resent the implication that you think he wants to, but he cannot resist "helping" someone he has learned to respect.

Local agents

Almost all Arab governments insist that you do business through a local agent, whether you are negotiating with a private business or with a government department. This policy has ensured lucrative careers and good incomes to Arab nationals and siphoned back some of the profits to the lands that generated them. It is a sound and sensible policy, very much in the national interests of the Arab countries.

You will not get far without a good Arab go-between. On a big deal, he can help you make the right contacts in the government, which you will need to get a decision to go ahead with the project. He will speed you through the paperwork (taking "speed" in a relative sense, of course), arrange for labor, materials, transport, storage, and accommodation and most importantly, expedite (less slowly than otherwise!) payments to you for your work.

A good local agent is more than somebody working for you; he is a partner in the venture and should be treated as such. He gets his income from commission (a percentage of the gross value of the deal), and he will expect to be consulted about everything. This may be far more than you normally disclose to your own employees, including, for example, your pricing policy.

Just how you handle this aspect of your relationship could influence greatly the energy with which he represents your interests in negotiations with other Arab nationals and government departments. It may appear that he is not doing a great deal for his commission (and the sum you pay to him can appear horrendous when said slowly, especially in comparison with your own earnings for creating the business), but without him you might find out just how bad Arab agents can be when they don't try very hard.

You will have to negotiate with him first about the level of his commission. This can range from 4 to 9 percent. (On a multimillion-dollar deal he is going to be very rich in no time.) Sure, you should still haggle for each percentage point or fraction of a point that he gets in commission. He will expect you to do so and might get suspicious if you don't.

You will find him accommodating in a negotiation. It will follow the same pace as the deals you will do with other nationals with him as a partner. "What will you be doing for our money?" is a useful question to keep on the table as you negotiate his commission, as is "What other major projects have you been agent for?"

Finding out what you are getting for your money is always a good idea in any negotiation. If you are not impressed with what is on offer you can lower his expectations of the price he will get for his services, or you can increase his commitments in return for what he gets.

Previous experience is another useful line of attack. If he was the go-between for a Japanese steel works or an American downstream processing plant, you have some assurance that he is worth what he is asking, and you have somewhere to go to check on his performance. If yours is his first big project, surely this is going to be reflected in his commission rate.

The ethics of commission and so on

You should pay for a go-between on a results-only basis. His commission is a percentage of the gross value of the business secured, not a commission on the gross value of the business you sought to get. You will want to ensure that if he does not

TIMES CHANGE

In 1958, a French car firm agreed to make an Arab businessman its agent in the Gulf. The Arab had approached them seeking an agency and had persuaded them that he had the acumen and the contacts to make the agency profitable.

The French negotiated an agency deal that required the Arab to pay in advance, every six months, for the cars they were about to ship out to him. They regarded this as a prudent necessity, to protect themselves in case the Arab failed to meet his commitments.

The requirement to pay in advance almost busted the Arab, as it meant that he had to borrow heavily from a local (foreign) bank that took a jaundiced view of lending large sums, on very little security, to local Arab nationals.

Over the years, however, the agency prospered, and the Arab sold a lot of cars at a profit and had a thriving spare parts business in support of his main operation.

After the 1973 oil price hike, when billions of dollars of income began to flow into the hands of the Gulf Arabs, the demand for cars rocketed. The Arab stood ready to make a great deal from his agency and his considerable experience in the market.

First, he took on the agency for a German car firm as well as the French one, and then he used the terms the Germans were delighted to offer him, in view of projected sales figures, as a basis for renegotiating the original deal he had with the French, who had no wish to be cut out of the lucrative Gulf market. He was able to renegotiate the agency deal to get cars on credit. From this point he expanded his agency rapidly.

The shift in market demand meant that the agency agreement held by the Arab in the lean years was now worth a lot more to the French car firm than it was to the now very rich Arab businessman.

He also set up his own local bank to manage the financial side of the agency and cut out the foreign bank that had given him a hard time on credit limits before 1973.

perform he does not get paid; anything else is for you a suicidal policy.

You can, if the state of the competition lets you, add his commission as a markup to your total charges to the client. You should remember that the commission of the competition's go-between will be a markup on their bid. If you can't do this, the commission will come out of your profits.

Of course, all this talk of a commission for a go-between to secure business for you through his contacts (perhaps somebody from his own extended family) hints at being slightly disreputable. Few people would exactly call it bribery, but it is close to a very narrow line between ethical and unethical business practices.

Now, it is not my objective to moralize about the business ethics of other countries or of foreigners like ourselves in them. The original purposes of the agency system were to give locals a piece of the action and to smooth the way for two cultures to become friends and do good business together. That original purpose is still present and is enshrined in the commercial laws of many Arab states, but like everything else it can get corrupted if it gets out of hand.

Is it a bribe to hire somebody on a performance contract to help you negotiate a deal with a government department and to help you supply what you have contracted to do if the deal is signed?

This is a very delicate legal question. If the agent induces somebody else for a reward (a cut out of his commission, say) *corruptly* to offer the business to his client (i.e., you), it seems to me that this is close to bribery of a third party by him, *if* the only reason that you got the business was the financial inducement that your agent offered. But are you corrupt in this transaction? Not if you are unaware of what your agent did. As far as you are concerned you paid the agent to help you to secure the business. What he does out of your sight and without your knowledge or instigation is not something you can be hauled up for—at least in theory!

Not all American courts, and not all Arab courts, either, have taken this view of those instances that have come to light (the Lockheed scandals or the Italian oil deals, for example). It is an offense in the United States to offer inducements corruptly to decision makers to favor you with business.

Insofar as your agent is not an officer of a decision-making structure—he is not a civil servant or officer of a purchasing company, for instance—he is not being bribed by you to secure business. If, however, he is a decision maker or, with your knowledge, is spreading his commission around to corrupt decision makers, then it is likely that you are engaged in corrupt practices.

How you handle a delicate situation like this, where you suspect you are implicated, innocently or otherwise, in bribery, is, of course, your own affair and not mine.

As long as you are clear in your own mind that you are paying a commission to a go-between for getting you to the negotiating carpet with Arab decision makers and are not paying him anything for going between you and the decision makers with a bag full of dollars, then you ought to be confident that your behavior will be of no interest to the courts. You can never be sure, though, that you are safe if you are operating in this rather murky area. Arab courts, for example, have not always been neutral or understanding even when senior figures have been charged with straying into bribery. President Sadat's brother was sent to jail for crossing the line between commission and bribery and so were several Western businessmen in Libya, Iraq, Iran, and Syria.

The worst thing you may say about your Arab go-between, even if he is half-decent at his job, is that he takes a long time to do it. On the surface this looks like a sign of inefficiency— of which you will no doubt get lots of other examples while you stay in hotels or travel around Arab countries.

On the other hand, it may be that you are pacing the deal

NO AGENTS HERE!

Not all Arab countries insist on a foreign firm's having an agent. In Iraq, for example, the government has decided on a deliberate policy of discouraging foreigners from dealing with government agencies through agents. The reasons have to do with the proclivity of the agent system to encourage corruption and the abuse of influence. Under socialist standards, agents who enrich themselves run counter to prevailing ethics, even if they act as honest go-betweens and in no way corrupt anybody. (In Egypt the government encourages agents but requires them to disclose their commission earnings and prohibits their being paid in accounts kept overseas.)

It is an offense in Iraq to use the services of an agent who is not formally registered with the public authorities. To do so risks being blacklisted by the government, preventing you from doing future business there. Moreover, even registered agents can be refused access to negotiations on your behalf in some state agencies.

This forces foreign companies to conduct their own search for business with the government. This involves formal documentation associated with tenders and bids, as well as a public statement that they support the boycott of Israel.

In such an atmosphere it is best to avoid dealing with anybody who claims to be able to throw a contract your way because of his alleged influence with somebody in the government service. You are unlikely to be given a contract as a result of his activities and are likely to end up with yourself, or officers from your company, in a local (unpleasant) jail.

In Saudi Arabia, in contrast, although local agents must register with the Ministry of Commerce, their role as intermediaries between Saudi purchasers (government or private) and foreign suppliers is directly encouraged. But take care in selecting an agent in most Arab countries. Once an agreement has been reached with a local national, it is extremely difficult to disengage from an agency relationship that has proved to be less than satisfactory, and the local courts are not models of objectivity in disputes between locals and foreigners.

too fast for the local community. He will spend not a little time socializing while engaged on your behalf in business with other Arabs. The delays that appear to be inflicted upon you will be inflicted upon him, with the difference that he will not be so acutely embarrassed by them as you might be.

The people he deals with have a different set of values from you. For instance, they will regard efficiency with less awe than you do, perhaps considering that loyalty from and to their Arab staff is more important.

Again, psychologically the Arab is out in the desert, alone with the people upon whom he depends for his very life. Loyalty when there is a water shortage is more important than efficiency. If you doubt this then you have never depended absolutely upon anybody for much that mattered.

The *bedu* is loyal, and he is learning about efficiency rather than practicing it. You should remember this in your dealings with your agent. Show loyalty to him and you will get it back in spades.

Alleged fatalism

Another carryover from this earlier age (not all that long past—thirty years ago the bedouin knew the true worth of a camel) is a sense of fatalism. This is a direct consequence of living on the edge of survival, where not much changes in the life-styles of successive generations. The cycle of life is not often interrupted by anything that man does. Nature holds dictatorial sway.

The rural societies of those who live close to nature tend to have a fatalistic view of the universe. "God wills" is an acknowledgment of man's weakness before the natural order of things. Once science is allied to man's needs, nature submits and with it the idea of fatalism.

When Americans witness Arabs in a fatalistic mood they

conclude that this is an essential characteristic of the Arab outlook on life. It is not, and a moment's reflection on the rural societies of Europe in previous centuries or the indigenous societies of North America would show this "fatalism" to be on a par with the superstition and myth of our own pasts. (How many Americans read their horoscopes each day?)

The modern Arab, the one you are likely to be negotiating with, is unlikely to leave his share of the deal to fate. You may take it for granted that he will work for the best deal for himself and leave nothing at all to chance.

Arab women

The perceptive reader will have noticed that this entire chapter has been written in the male gender, as if the female did not exist. This might have antagonized feminists. It has been, however, a deliberate policy on my part to exclude from the chapter any reference to Arab women until now.

It is not that the Arab woman does not count; of course she does, in her society. But unless you are mixing business with cultural reform (a short-term activity in the Middle East), the position and the future of Arab women is, to be pretty blunt about it, none of your damn business!

Old hands in the Middle East always advise outsiders to steer well clear of even the thought of Arab women while visiting Arab countries. They do so, for good reason. Arabs do not like interference in their private affairs by foreigners, especially those who know little of what they are talking about.

If you want to join the League for Stirring Up Trouble in Arab Countries, you may go ahead and state your views to whoever will listen to you. You will not, however, be able to combine such activity with doing business with Arabs.

I was once saved at a dinner party in Houston from an indiscretion in talking about the subject of Arab women in their homelands. My guests were an Egyptian Arab and his wife, and during the evening I raised the subject of the Arab attitude to women in conversation.

The reply I got came not from the man but from his wife, an articulate educated woman, who spoke better English than I did Arabic and who knew both the American and Arab societies from having lived in both since she was a schoolgirl. Her defense of her status within her Arab family left me realizing that I knew nothing at all about the issues involved, and I resolved never to raise the subject again. I suggest you do the same.

In some countries, Arab women play an increasingly important and public role in government, business, and political affairs. In others, there is a long way to go before they will achieve even limited recognition outside of their immediate families. This may or may not be enough to encourage you to accept that other people live the way they do because it suits them. If it doesn't suit them, only they can change it.

In all Arab countries you would do well to concern yourself with what you came to do, namely to negotiate with your Arab counterpart. This means, in the main everywhere and exclusively in some countries, that you will do business with a man. If you resent this, or can't accept it, you are unlikely to do business at all.

Hence, if you are a man, do not even think about women in Arab countries, let alone attempt to importune them, innocently or otherwise. If you must look at a camel, as I was advised in Muscat by an ex-officer of the Arab Legion, "Make sure it is a male one!"

Women negotiators—an unlikely phenomenon in an Arab country—should be wary of flirting even innocently with a male, especially in a public place. Local people are easily roused to anger by any immodesty on the part of a female

TIPS FOR TRAVELERS IN THE MIDDLE EAST

Check the labels on all the clothes that you are taking with you, including the ones that you are wearing for the journey. Remove any labels from any store that could be on the Arab boycott list. Customs officers vary in the diligence with which they scan the labels to look for "Jewish" products. It might be best if you took all labels off everything, just in case they might confiscate your clothes on arrival. (Note that your being in transit is no protection.)

In view of Arab sensitivity in matters connected with the state of Israel, do not attempt to travel to Arab countries with an Israeli visa stamp anywhere in your passport. You can either persuade the Israeli immigration official not to stamp your passport at all or you can apply for two passports, one for use on visits to Israel and the other for visits to the Arab countries. The Israelis normally do not care if your passport is stamped by the Arab states.

Jewish citizens of the United States are not normally harassed by the Arab authorities, but Israeli citizens should check with their own authorities as to which countries are safe for them.

The Middle East has more than its share of sensitive political conflicts going on at any moment. Hence, avoid all discussions of politics, especially if you think you know something about the particular issue and absolutely if you know nothing about it!

Do not get into situations where you are flouting local laws, especially in matters of alcohol. Watch out for expatriates who invite you to drinking parties in Saudi. The booze is doubly dangerous—it's likely to be almost pure alcohol, and the police might arrive.

People who try to smuggle drugs in Turkey can spend a long time in an unpleasant jail. In Iran, they might even execute you. In fact, my travel tip for those contemplating a trip to Iran is—don't.

Do not conduct yourself as if you have no respect for local manners; they might deport you out of the country. Immodest dress by females is highly dangerous. Disrespect to local women by males is suicidal.

and could get apoplectic with rage at a public pass or hint of sexual preference. In these circumstances you can regard how you handle a pass from an Arab male as supreme test of your professionalism.

ANSWERS TO SELF-ASSESSMENT TEST 5

1 You must arrange to take as much time as is available to you if you intend to conduct business with Arabs. If your time is short (seven days) only go to one country. If you must visit them all, take at least thirty-one days and if possible, another two weeks. [For anything less than twenty-eight days deduct 10 points; for twenty-eight days and over add 10 points.]

2 a Never! Do not introduce a business subject with an Arab under any circumstances. Even if he is visiting you, wait for him to raise the subject. If he is visiting you in the United States, wait for some considerable time before bringing up the subject and do so only after you have exhausted your small talk. Never appear in a hurry to talk business and never ever appear irritated by the lack of progress in this area.   (−10)

b Yes.   (10)

3 a Yes. A sign of your respect for him.   (10)

b No. It's too obvious an attempt on your part to hustle him into discussing business with you before he is ready.   (−10)

c Absolutely not! This suggests that you are annoyed and that he is a poor host. Stick to *a* and let business take its own course.   (−20)

CHAPTER **6**

Similarity in Diversity—or, Doing Deals South of the Rio Grande

Slow down

If citizens of the United States seldom take a long time to do a deal, citizens of the Americas south of the Rio Grande seldom do a deal, or much else, quickly, and if there is one thing that they dislike, it is being pushed around or rushed by "wham, bam, it's a deal, Sam" negotiators from the North.

While you as a North American are rushing into plans, South Americans are still trying to get to know you. When you are thinking in billions, or even trillions, they are thinking in millions, or perhaps hundreds of thousands. While you want to sign up the entire continent for your wonderful products, they concern themselves with the minute portion they can handle within their national territory. Some U.S. companies have total world sales greater than the GNPs of some South American countries.

You are going to have to slow down the pace of your negotiations or attempts at negotiation with business managers in Central and South America and probably scale down your volume numbers, too.

It's always difficult coming from a large country to a smaller one. There is natural irritation (seldom disguised by

[test appears on following page]

113

SELF-ASSESSMENT TEST 6

1 You have a Ph.D. in Latin American history, and you are engaged in social conversation with your business partners in Bogotá. The discussion drifts to the subject of Latin American economic development. Do you:

a Avail yourself of the opportunity to discourse briefly on the comparative social and political differences between North and South America in the nineteenth century?

b Ask your partners for their views but offer none yourself?

c Ask them why they think California and other former regions of Mexico have done so well as part of the United States, compared to their mother country?

d Suggest that South America needs social and political reforms to generate successful capitalism on U.S. lines?

2 You are in Rio de Janeiro making preliminary inquiries into selecting a local agent for your laser metal-cutting machines. You speak poor Spanish. Do you:

a Make an attempt to speak Spanish to your contacts?

b Refrain from doing so and concentrate solely on English?

3 You are looking for ways to sell your products in Venezuela, and you are approached by a merchant in Caracas who offers to represent you in the entire country. Do you:

a Sign a contract with him after checking out his financial standing?

b Ask him who else he represents?

being patronizing) at a person who thinks smaller than you do, but remember the guy thinks smaller because he and his business opportunities are smaller. It's probably more difficult for a deal to be struck between a negotiator in Bolivia and a negotiator in Chile than it is for you to visit both places and do two separate deals.

If you take your time and learn to slow down the pace of your business life, you will probably end up doing more business than you will if you don't.

Save your high energy output for the tiring flight between Mexico City and Ezeiza airport, Buenos Aires. Save your breath for your business trip to La Paz in Bolivia, where you'll need it just for the journey from the taxi to the lobby of the Plaza hotel. (You're 12,500 feet above sea level, and you will feel as if you have jogged all the way from El Alto airport carrying your bag—two bags will kill you!)

Don't look down

Above all else, learn to avoid giving the impression that you are doing them a favor by offering them deals in the first place.

People south of the Rio Grande have an ambivalent attitude to the United States. They admire, indeed covet, its material wealth but don't have much time for what they regard as the insensitivity, almost arrogance, of some of its citizens with whom they come into contact. (This insensitivity is not confined to U.S. citizens. Many Europeans are just as bad, if not even more appalling, in their business manners, and more than one deal has died as a result.)

Negative perceptions about the United States are often unfair, but they are nevertheless widespread. Latin Americans are very proud of their national identities. Their countries may well be poorer than the United States, their political systems may often be less than democratic, their performance compared to America's in the years since the sixteenth century may not cast them in the best light, and their people may be sharply divided into haves and have-nots on a scale seen nowhere here, but they are emotionally attached to their countries, manifest failings and all, with a passion no less deeply felt than the pride of the most red-blooded of U.S. patriots in the U.S. Constitution and America's manifest successes.

It can require a considerable effort on the part of some U.S. negotiators approaching business deals in Central and South America for the first time to set aside their innocent unintended biases and their predetermined stereotypes and treat the people with whom they hope to do business with the respect and equality that they deserve and seek. Almost without being conscious of it, U.S. first timers (and not a few of the old hands) can slip into attitudes and let fall verbal asides that rub the Latin American the wrong way, much to the detriment of the business that they might have done if a more sensitive posture had been even half as obvious as their rude one.

Don't look back

South Americans do not take kindly to lectures by North Americans (or Europeans) on how they might have done it all better if only they had done it the same way as the pioneers in the North. They are well aware that the social and political institutions of South America have not always helped its development processes, but they are just as aware that these social and political institutions are part of their country's heritage, for good or evil, and are as valuable to their societies as social stabilizers as are those institutions that are revered by people in the United States. Some of their capital cities were founded before the Pilgrim Fathers had the first Thanksgiving dinner with the local Indians.

South Americans do not regard their pasts with unmitigated shame and resent having often incorrect versions of their history shoved down their throats—even politely—by people who have as much guilt about the North American Indian and the black slave trade as they are alleged to about their Indians. It is salutary to note that many of the people of these countries are pure-blood Indians or mixed Indian and Spanish (as in Bolivia, Colombia, Peru, Paraguay, and Venezuela), and these proud peoples have demonstrated an ethnic integration and survival rate that compares remarkably well with that of the indigenous peoples of North America.

Every ethnic mix is found in South America. The proportion of European stock runs from the almost totally European populations of Argentina and Uruguay through Brazil's 60 percent to Chile's 30 percent, Venezuela's 20 percent, and Peru's 11 percent. The mix includes pure-blooded Amerindians, mestizos (mixed Spanish and Indian), Creoles (part African descent), Asian Indians, and mulattoes.

If you are doing business in South America you could be negotiating with someone from almost any racial group. If you remember that you are the outsider, the "foreigner," the "gringo" (and some Latins can say "gringo" in a way that makes clear they have been insulted in the past by another gringo), you will have no difficulty on racial grounds.

The men or (less likely) the women with whom you are negotiating, whatever their racial origins or mixtures, are at home in their society. Because they will be rich by definition—only the rich negotiate with the business gringos, for only the rich have the wherewithal to do a deal—they will be respected in their societies for being rich, if for nothing else. It's not the color of skins that counts in Latin America, it's wealth and position.

WITH FRIENDS LIKE THESE ...

An Argentinian business leader was visiting Capitol Hill to meet with various senators who were in favor of strong U.S.–Argentinian relations. He met with the staff of one senator who had long been prominent in promoting good relations between U.S. and Argentinian business leaders.

It was not long before the subject of the Argentinian economy came up and the high rate of inflation that was afflicting it. The Argentinian explained the political and economic background of his country's inflation problems and dealt with the legacy of the Peron years and how the military governments had not been very competent in dealing with the real issues.

A member of the senator's staff told the visitor, "If we could run your country for eighteen months, we would soon turn it around." He took the silence that followed as an invitation to continue with his thoughts on how the United States would run Argentina better than the Argentinians.

He did not know it then (though the senator made it abundantly clear later), but making such statements was likely to do more damage to U.S.–Argentinian relations in ten minutes than some critics of Argentina could manage in a lifetime. And no amount of reference by the senator's aide to the Falklands as the Malvinas compensated for the derogatory implications of his remarks.

Argentinians, in common with most people everywhere else, including North Americans, do not take kindly to foreigners who insult them. Of course, people who understand their own country's problems and are honest enough to talk about them with foreigners risk, though they do not invite, ignorant know-it-alls telling them how much better they could run their economies in "eighteen months."

But for a so-called friend of Argentina to make this mistake shows just how easy it is to sink a negotiation by thoughtless remarks.

Mind your own business

On the economic front, a country like Brazil, where whatever else occasionally torments its people racism does not, if it follows present trends will become one of the world's top five economies as measured by GNP. Mexico, Argentina, and Venezuela, whatever the problems of the past, are by no means excluded from a sound economic future, and they have much to be proud of (and know it) in what they have achieved already. In sum, the twenty-first century may well be the time when Latin America comes into its own.

At present you are negotiating with people who live on a continent of nations diverse in circumstance, environment, and outlook, yet similar in history, opportunity, and way of life.

The legacy of the two European powers, Spain and Portugal, that colonized the greater part of the continent is everywhere to be seen in the languages spoken (Portuguese in Brazil, Spanish everywhere else, albeit with a local hemispheric intonation) and in the institution of the Roman Catholic Church (with tolerated "adds-ons" from indigenous Indian and slave trade peoples' religions). Similar legacies of the past on a much smaller scale can be seen in the French, Dutch, and British former colonies of Central and South America and the Caribbean islands.

The South American political structure is a Latin, and therefore manqué, version of the American revolution against European colonialism. The early nineteenth century independence revolutions against Spain and Portugal did not lead to a United States of South America, despite the hopes of such as Simón Bolívar, but led instead to a score of separate nation-states, each duplicating the apparatus of statehood (armed forces, customs barriers, state currencies, legal systems) and foregoing the benefits of a large market (free trade in goods and free movement of peoples).

With this background in mind, keep your views on the world to yourself and above all else, mind your own business about how they run their country. You are out to trade your goods for dollars, or vice versa, not to embark on a career as a nation reformer. The first task is difficult enough, the latter futile. You might as well try to sell booze and pork cutlets to the Arabs as interfere gratuitously in the politics of a South American country. You are there to negotiate for your business, not to take sides.

Anyway, there are radicals aplenty trying to change South America from the inside (they live there!), and nobody needs advice from you on how to run things "better." If you're interested in politics, run for office in the United States; don't try to combine this with a business career in South America.

Moreover, and this is pure Latin American, many members of the richer layers of the societies, with whom you might be negotiating, favor various degrees of change in the way their countries run their affairs, too. You can never be sure that the guy you are mouthing off at is not sympathetic to the very changes taking place in his country that you are denouncing.

You are there to do business, so keep to that agenda. Otherwise you may end up being told whose business to mind and how far away in the world you should mind it.

Less than free trade

One great and immediately obvious contrast between doing business in South America and doing business in the United States is the consequence of a continent consisting of thirteen separate countries (or twenty-one if Central America and thirty-four if the Caribbean are included) instead of just two.

A Texan wanting to export his products to any of the states of America need do no more than comply with the same federal laws that govern him in Texas (with minor differences in state zoning and taxation, perhaps). He will also get paid in the same currency in which he pays his own employees, the U.S. dollar.

The same Texan business that wants to export its products south of the Rio Grande will have to confront twenty-one different sets of commercial laws and regulations, twenty-one different taxation systems, and twenty-one different customs procedures.

If he manages to get paid in U.S. dollars he will still have to convert his prices into local currencies, some of which sound the same but aren't (for example, pesos in Bolivia, Chile, Colombia, Uruguay, and Argentina) and some of which don't and still aren't (the bolivar in Venezuela, guarani in Paraguay, sol in Peru, sucre in Ecuador, and cruzeiro in Brazil). There are also some that sound familiar (the franc in French Guiana, dollar in Guyana, and guilder in Surinam).

Foreign currencies are a bewildering topic even to bankers. If different rates of domestic inflation are taken into account, the exchange rates between foreign currencies and the dollar are additionally complicated, and this can have some significance for a U.S. business in negotiating a deal.

A million dollars of electrical switch gear has a different value to an exporter if the deal is cost, insurance, and freight (CIF) to a warehouse in Buenaventura in Colombia instead of free on board (FOB), San Francisco.

This problem is compounded if the CIF price is quoted to a place like Rosario in Argentina where inflation has recently been hitting 400 percent a year. Inflation-ridden port labor charges alone could make a good profit marginal unless compensated for by severe and frequent devaluations of the peso against the dollar.

This gives international negotiators something else to think about on top of the many other things they must consider. It's not just the dollar price that is important, it's where and when it becomes due and at what exchange rate and who pays for associated services in other currencies.

From a U.S. negotiator's point of view, the deal should be denominated in U.S. dollars, leaving inflationary and exchange rate fluctuations as a problem exclusively for the other guy. It should also be fixed in FOB terms, leaving shipping costs for the importer or to the shipping company.

Customs regulations in some countries (such as Brazil) will assess tariff rates on the CIF value of the goods irrespective of trading terms. If they catch you, or suspect you of, "mistakenly" undervaluing your goods you could be penalized by a doubling of the tariff duty. In some countries you must enter the CIF and the FOB prices on the invoice regardless of who is paying the difference.

But whatever happens, a U.S. negotiator must keep the deal in U.S. dollars. Bags full of a foreign currency may sound OK at today's exchange rate but be nothing but bags full of paper in a year's time.

Naturally, members of the business community of South America have alerted their governments to the vagaries of international trade. These governments have passed laws that aim to assist their own negotiators—though their net effect is to restrain trade.

Generally, imports are regarded by the protectionist-minded as less attractive than exports. (Free trade is less than free, and nowhere is this more true than in South America.) Commercial regulations based on this prejudice always end up, whatever the intentions of the legislators, inhibiting trade. Such proposals are *always* presented as being in the national interest, but always and everywhere they are in the interests of a minority of businesspeople.

Paperwork as an import barrier

Whole batteries of import license regulations exist in several countries, and they will be fired off at you no matter how big a favor you think you are doing to a country by selling it advanced technology and products that will do it nothing but good.

You can get your goods to the port in, say, Colombia and still not get them through customs until stringent formalities are completed. In truth you have little to complain about, because U.S. Customs is formality ridden too, but then the United States is almost self-sufficient at a high income level while all of Latin America is the exact opposite—self-deficient at low income levels.

Typically, and not the least of it, your opposite number will have to pay into his country's central bank between 40 and 60 percent of the peso value of the goods you are selling to him. That is just to get the goods out of customs and into his hands.

From his side of the negotiating table this legal requirement for a prior deposit acts to inhibit him from importing goods that he is not fairly sure of selling. This thus inhibits the taking of risks and the entrepreneurial seizure of opportunities. As he can never be sure of selling anything in advance, he must put pressure on your prices and has every incentive to do so, apart from this being a basic negotiating stance common the world over.

The import deposit law precludes him from making advance payments to you. He would be crazy to agree to dollar deposits or payments on account unless you accepted payment in his local currency, which would suggest you were crazy too, or certainly desperate. His country's laws push him into a tough bargaining stance whether he is temperamentally geared for one or not—and South Americans can be just as astute as you when it comes to the terms of your mutual deal.

HEAR THIS, IMPORTERS!

Many Latin American countries actively discourage imports. Just to make sure that you and your potential partners get the message, the country's government will give you the prospect of paying all kinds of taxes just for the privilege of selling goods to people who want to buy them but not at any price.

Brazil is a classic example of the application of disincentives to import (Mexico was for a long time another example). Assuming your products are not on the long list of "national similars" (things that can be produced in Brazil), they would be liable to the following duties before you can sell them to the otherwise happy Brazilians.

1 A tariff ad valorem on the CIF value decided on by a government customs official (i.e., not by you or your Brazilian partner).

2 A tax on the foreign exchange transaction required by your Brazilian partner if he was to pay in dollars.

3 A federal manufactured goods tax calculated on the "duty paid," not CIF, value.

4 A state merchandise circulation tax calculated on the duty plus all other taxes paid value.

5 A 3 percent ad valorem port charge (which, thank goodness, included the "Port Improvement Tax").

6 A 2 percent ad valorem CIF warehousing charge, plus all customs inspection and paperwork expenses.

7 A 20 percent of the cost of freight charge to the Merchant Marine Fund.

8 A 2 percent ad valorem CIF customs broker's commission.

9 Finally, a levy of 10 percent on the customs broker's commission to be paid to the broker's union.

Meanwhile, your goods are sitting in a South American warehouse, and you have not yet been paid a cent. The risk for title to your goods is carried by you, and there is not a lot you can do about it. If you decide not to take such a risk— and you are always free so to do—you will trade elsewhere, which is what is intended by those who promoted these trading laws (and variations on them found around the world).

You won't get closer to getting paid unless and until your trading partner deposits at his state bank various certificates, including the import license he should have obtained before ordering the goods (did he do this?), your invoice (which must have absolutely no mistakes on it, even typographical ones, so make sure your Spanish translation is perfect), and a letter from him, countersigned by his bank, that he owes you the dollar value of the goods you have sent to him.

But you still don't get your money! About three weeks later, the importer applies to the exchange registration office (or equivalent in his country) for a license to pay you in dollars. In several more weeks—or even longer!—he should receive permission to purchase foreign exchange for remittance to you.

He will now have to pay his bank its commission for handling the transaction and the balance owing on the goods above the deposit he made perhaps several months earlier when they arrived at his country's port; that is, when you completed your end of the deal.

As a negotiator you are boxed in to some extent. Not only can you not get him to agree to pay you in advance, even a small deposit, but you cannot hold onto title to your goods once he applies to clear them through customs. How fast he sells them in his country is not in your hands, but his, and naturally if sales are sluggish he has an incentive not to process the import documentation and exchange formalities as fast as you might be anxious for him to do so.

You can opt for a letter of credit type of transaction, but

this will cost you bank charges for arranging it. It will also be fixed at a minimum of 90 days. The question as to which way you are paid fastest is something only hindsight will tell you!

Try padding your prices

I would not go so far as to suggest that every deal you make is subject to "administrative" delays which cover up your partner's (temporary) commercial embarrassments, but you certainly are vulnerable to these delays. Therefore you must seek to negotiate deals only with the soundest of business partners. This usually means large rather than small South American businesses and products that have a fairly certain demand, such as high-value machinery for a government contract, preferably one that has some "political protection" and U.S. diplomatic leverage close to it.

The worst thing for you to do when faced with delays is to agree to renegotiate the price of the deal, just to get some of your money. There is a temptation to do so—not that they need suggest this to you. You would not be worth much as a businessman if you did not automatically think of this option when reading the above paragraphs.

But selling cheap to get paid is your last resort, not a regular option, and if undertaken under duress it must be a prelude to getting out of a Latin American line of business altogether.

In fact, knowing that there is going to be this kind of pressure on you while you are waiting for your money suggests that you should be padding your prices beforehand to ensure that you are paid for being your partner's banker.

But price padding, of course, makes you less competitive, and there is plenty of competition around. You are thus likely to be inhibited from fully covering your risks and implicit credit costs.

One thing that must be obvious is that price cutting to get business is a short-term strategy for trade with South America (or, for that matter, anywhere else). If you strip your prices by shaving your profit you will end up with losses.

You are also likely to end up with losses if you charge only your normal rates when trading into administratively difficult places. Also, you are unlikely to make a worthwhile profit if you deal in small quantities of low-value items. Hence, don't.

Using somebody else's money

Trade with Latin America has to be in big-league quantities of goods and services, which probably means that you will be dealing with major trading partners (perhaps local subsidiaries of multinational companies) or with the country's government.

If the vagaries of getting paid by your importing partner worry you enough for you to seek business elsewhere, you might want to consider getting into the relatively secure business of trading with South American countries for money that belongs neither to you nor the country you are trading with.

Almost every day of every year, some development agency in the world approves economic aid to one developing country or another, and the benefits of access to these funds are sufficient inducement for South American governments to relish their countries being classed as "developing."

The benefit of a development grant for a U.S. company lies in the fact that you get paid by the agency (the World Bank or whatever) for sending your products to the country concerned. You do not have to await the results of the ponderous administrative procedures of the country's customs office or its financial institutions. If the World Bank grants you a contract to supply Argentina with your products you can take it that your bank account will be credited with U.S. dollars without hassle.

In fact, a quick sweep of the various development agencies that finance such deals, including the local field offices of these agencies located in South America, could provide you with your initial sales leads. Aid agencies publish regular lists of tenders you can bid for, and personal contact on the spot could be the start of a useful relationship. Being seen in the country by people able to point you in the direction of government agencies seeking to import your kinds of products is better than sending them a letter even in flawless Spanish (or Portuguese), though that is better than waiting for them to contact you!

Getting your products to the aid agency's attention may initiate the process by which the local office of the agency prompts the relevant local department to get its government to approach the Washington head office of the agency to finance a deal to buy your products. It sounds complicated, but more than one multimillion-dollar deal has begun with a U.S. negotiator calling at a local aid agency office and getting to know the guy behind the desk where the aid deals are first put together.

Finding an agent

Much of the international trade with Latin America that is not financed by world aid agencies or that does not involve direct dealings with the government or a state-owned company is promoted by some version of the agency system.

Some governments encourage foreign companies to set up manufacturing subsidiaries in partnership with nationals inside the country. They mainly do this by discouraging imports. Where this is not commercially suitable for your business—too small a local market, for instance—you have no alternative but to arrange to import your goods into the country. For this you will need a local agent.

You can try sending out your own resident representative, but even he will have to deal through a network of local agents or somebody who has, or claims to have, such a network working for him.

Your first negotiation in South America is likely to be with the national who desires (though he may not give you that impression by his demeanor) to be your officially appointed agent. Agents the world over are of two kinds: those who work for you all the time and those who work for you some of the time (if at all).

Care, of course, must be taken to select a good agent, but this is easier said than done. He might claim to have representatives in every corner of Brazil, and he can certainly produce expense claims that suggest he has an army of subagents working for him out of the best suites at the Rio Sheraton, but you need to check his claims thoroughly. You need coverage all over Brazil or at least in Rio de Janeiro, São Paulo, and Minas Gerais (and perhaps the duty-free zone of Manaus).

Getting rid of a bad agent is not easy, and local laws exist in some, but thank goodness not all, South American countries to discourage the consequences of your outrage when you find him sitting on a warehouse full of your goods with not a paid invoice in sight.

Suing him in, say, Venezuela or Ecuador will cost you a small fortune, because his country's laws work for him and not for you, the foreigner. He's also likely to be entitled to compensation for your "arbitrary" dismissal. (Remember, local courts the world over define almost any dismissal of one of their countrymen as arbitrary.)

On the other hand, in Uruguay you can sack an agent without risk of a damaging compensation dispute, but the stakes you are likely to be trading for in Uruguay compared

RUM DEALS IN THE POOL

A vice-president of a U.S. beer company was on a business tour of South America and was telexed by his head office to go to Jamaica on his way back to meet with the management team of one of the local rum exporters. His problem was that he did not have the business work permit required for a business visit to Jamaica, nor did he have time to acquire one on his tight schedule.

Hence, he went into Norman Manley airport, Kingston, as a tourist. His problems began at immigration, because it was obvious from his previous itinerary and correspondence in his briefcase that he had been on a business trip. He claimed to the officials that he was in Jamaica for a few days' recreation before returning to Milwaukee.

He booked into his hotel and phoned the rum exporter he wanted to meet. Later at the hotel he was interviewed by an immigration official who accused him of being in Jamaica for business purposes without a proper work permit. The official told him that he was being watched and that if he did any business at all he would be arrested, fined heavily, and deported.

For two days the policeman shadowed him everywhere and forced him to spend the days and evenings like a tourist. The visit was clearly going to be a waste of time and money.

Before leaving, however, he met with the rum exporter, and they did a deal right under the nose of the police.

The hotel had a bar in the pool which swimmers could sit beside while in the water. While a policeman sat keeping a sleepy eye on him, he sat at the bar in the pool talking to the bartender and a young woman who joined them.

The policeman assumed that he was merely idling away his time talking to a bartender and flirting with a guest. In fact, he was negotiating with the head of the rum company, who was behind the bar dressed as a bartender. His secretary was the "guest" undressed in a bikini in the pool.

Moral: Initiative can beat any bureaucratic nonsense aimed at stopping people doing business.

to Venezuela are likely to be so small as to hardly make it worth the telex fee to sack him. In Peru the law, surprisingly, supports you against the local agent.

To get the agent position sorted out—and you must do so for your own best interests—you will have to get into the field, perhaps putting one of your own people in residence (make sure he or she speaks Portuguese in Brazil and Spanish everywhere else), and negotiate good incentive terms that will make the agent work for your products and not your rivals'. (Check that he is not an agent for all the leading brands in your field, if only to protect your negotiating flanks.)

Check out the local laws. For example, in Brazil you will be liable for Brazilian profits tax if your agent can bind you to a deal he makes with a third party, while in Venezuela it has to be pretty clear that your agent is your representative.

Your negotiating objectives must be to make the contract with the agent specific about what he can and cannot do in your name and what entitlements he has to orders he generates himself and to those that come to you without his intervention.

Ideally, you want him tied to sales targets, with clear performance standards as a guide to contract termination or renewal. Realistically, where there are more foreign vendors than local agents (as in Venezuela, for instance), you may simply be getting a deal that gets your products into an agent's distribution system with no guarantees at all that he will push your interests among all his other obligations.

Business manners

The way business is conducted in a country reflects its social mores. This results in a manageable variation of business manners in South and Central America. Broadly, Latin

America is a combination of Mediterranean and indigenous culture. There is a very little that is naturally Northern European in its business style. Typically, for example, it is said of the Argentinians that they are Italians who speak Spanish and think they are English (except, of course, in matters related to the Malvinas!).

Argentinians are certainly more formal than most of their continental neighbors. Buenos Aires (or "B.A."—as in "L.A."—to the resident English speakers) is a very European city. Its residents share with those of many European countries the habit of incessantly shaking hands at every opportunity. (Make sure you are ready to shake hands wherever you go in South America. It is the absolutely minimum symbol of good manners and respect.)

Brazilians have a reputation for fun loving—the world-famous Copacabana beach is only one of several near Rio de Janeiro where the sensuous indulge their hedonism—and they wholly deserve what they enjoy. In business matters the Brazilian works on an interpersonal level. If he likes you he will do business with you, but even then he will not let business get in the way of his leisure. (So avoid trying to open negotiations during Carnival—for one thing, the din is so loud you wouldn't hear what was being said!)

Chile, Paraguay, Uruguay, and Colombia are very conservative places in which to do business. Politeness, including correct forms of address (and correct forms of dress), is mandatory. Don't turn up for negotiations wearing the clothes you would in Malibu. Stick to a business suit, lightweight if necessary, but conservative at all times.

In Peru they are positively Italian or Greek in their disregard for punctuality, and in Ecuador do not expect anybody to keep an appointment until you are actually shaking his or her hand (and even then you may be greeting an apologetic messenger). Benign, not irritated, persistence is required, particularly with government negotiators.

TIPS FOR TRAVELERS IN SOUTH AMERICA

Thieves (and worse) are endemic in Belize City, Belize; in Bogotá, Colombia (the "thieves' capital of the world"); and in Georgetown, Guyana. It's also risky after dark in Kingston, Jamaica. In Panama City, Panama, avoid sellers of anything. Daylight thieves abound in Mexico City, Mexico, but in Quito, Ecuador, they mainly work the night shift. Rio de Janeiro during Carnival is a wonderful social occasion, but it can be dangerous; in 1985 ninety-six people were killed in four days of the world's longest samba.

Personal safety and security of property are more or less assured in Buenos Aires, Argentina (though always refer to the Falklands as the Malvinas); in Montevideo, Uruguay (keep off politics altogether); and in Santiago, Chile (not a good place for political seminars either).

Venezuela reveres Simón Bolívar, who liberated it and neighboring countries from the Spanish. Be extremely respectful about Bolívar statues and places named after him. It is useful to remember that in Caracas there are four rush hours, the usual two plus two more to accommodate the penchant of *caraquenos* for siesta.

Venezuelan taxi drivers do not automatically accept a fare—they may haggle with you about whether they are going to take you at all (and they frequently get lost themselves in the jumbled unmarked streets of the city). Similarly, in Brazil assume the taxi driver is a total stranger in the city, and get the hotel porter to give him precise directions.

Don't visit La Paz, Bolivia, if you have a respiratory or heart complaint. The high altitude (over 12,000 feet) is exhausting to a fit person and positively lethal to the rest of us. Note: La Paz is not the sort of city you go to for an *affair de coeur*, not unless it's a mutual suicide pact. Try Rio de Janeiro instead.

Brazilian visa regulations for business negotiators are notorious for their complexity; hence, go on a tourist visa. For other countries check with your travel agent.

It is incumbent upon you, the foreigner, to make and confirm your appointments and to turn up on time for them. The vagueness about time keeping is a characteristic reserved for the national concerned, and you had better not "go native" and indulge in it yourself just in case your opposite number takes offense at your insensitivity.

Finally, remember that while the nations of Central and South America have a great deal in common—the similarities they share—they are also extremely diverse and fiercely determined to keep it that way.

If you refrain from interfering in the social structures, keep your views on how the world is best run to yourself (no comments are advisable on how local army squads might be going about their sometimes assertive business), and have the patience to learn about the pace of business in the country you are visiting, you will be well on your way to establishing the personal relationships essential for doing business with a Latin American.

If you forget this advice, you will be just another unsuccessful Yankee or worse, a boorish gringo. You'll look even more unsuccessful when your people send down in your place one of your colleagues who gets it right and does the business that eluded you because you forgot your business manners and what you were there for.

ANSWERS TO SELF-ASSESSMENT TEST 6

1 a Not if you want to do business with people who are somewhat sensitive to foreigners lecturing them on their past. Your Ph.D. is of interest only to you, your college, and perhaps your mother. **(−10)**
b The wisest choice. It gets them talking about the subject: what makes their country tick and what doesn't, which they know more about than you do. And even if they are wrong, it's their history, and they won't take kindly to you telling them otherwise. **(10)**

c You are of a suicidal disposition! If you mention this in Mexico you deserve Montezuma's revenge. (−20)

d Still an appalling arrogance on your part, especially if you detail the reforms you think are necessary. Stay off politics, history, and reforms. (−15)

2 a While many Brazilians understand Spanish they seldom if ever speak it. They speak Portuguese and would think you irritating if you did not know the difference. (−10)

b Yes. It's better to speak English, even through an interpreter, than Spanish if you do not know (Brazilian) Portuguese. (10)

3 a His financial standing, while important, is not enough background on him and his business for you to sign a contract. It only tells you that he has financial resources; you want to know if he can market your goods. (−10)

b Yes. It is essential that you find out if he is going to represent you exclusively or you and your rivals. If he is serving your competitors too, what negotiating position do you think this puts him in? Moreover, does he have facilities outside Caracas to sell your products? (10)

SELF-ASSESSMENT TEST 7

1 You are visiting China for the first time in order to discuss with the National Machinery Import and Export Corporation (MA-CHIMPEX) the sale of heavy duty pumps. They inform you that China needs to replace 100,000 pumps over the next five years. They tell you that initially they want to buy five of your pumps (which you sell around the world for about 19,000 dollars each) and that if your price is lower than your competitor's you could get the order. Do you:

a Go in at a price of 19,000 dollars?

b Give them a large "trial" discount to get your five pumps into China with a view to the follow-up orders for the 100,000 they need later?

c Quote a price per pump of 23,500 dollars?

2 You are negotiating with the China National Cereals, Oils and Foodstuffs Import and Export Corporation to import from China various traditional foodstuffs. What do you expect them to agree to in respect to payment?

a Payment in hard currency on your receipt of the goods

b Payment in hard currency on the dispatch of the goods

c Payment in hard currency at a date to be agreed on, loosely related to the actual dispatch of the goods

3 You are in the export-import business. In Peking, the authorities offer you the use of letter of credit facilities to cover transactions with the Chinese foreign trade corporations. These facilities allow for "irrevocable, transferable and divisible" letters of credit through the Bank of China. Do you expect the same terms and obligations to apply for both exports (where they are the payers) and imports (where you are the payer)?

a Yes

b No

CHAPTER 7

The Scrutable Chinese—or, How They Do Business in Peking

Soviet-style trade monopoly

The Chinese have based their foreign trade system on that of the Soviet Union. It is very Stalinist in scope and content. Much that has been discussed in chapter 3 applies to the conduct of commercial negotiations with representatives of the People's Republic of China (PRC). Recent developments in China, combined with its divergence from the Soviet Union over the past twenty-five years, however, have produced variations in the Soviet-style system that are important and are more than mere nuances of emphasis. For a start, there is now greater scope for foreign businesses to negotiate trade deals with the Chinese state bureaucracy and greater willingness on China's part, if it suits the current requirements of the Chinese economy, to seek out appropriate business deals with American firms.

Much, however, remains familiar. Bureaucratic delays, endless reviews by a labyrinth of committees, hard bargaining on prices and performance guarantees, and a general (though sometimes genial) atmosphere of semisuspicion at the motives of outsiders characterize business negotiations with the PRC.

The purpose of China's monopoly of foreign trade system is similar to that of the Soviet Union's. It is an instrument for maintaining the absolute leading role of the Communist party in all aspects of the relationship of its citizens with the outside world. In addition, the system has the economic effect of ensuring that trade does not interfere with the centralized state economic plan; citizens pursuing their own ventures with foreigners is incompatible with a planned economy.

The foreign trade organization (FTO) handles everything in connection with the proposed business transaction, and this, in the main, precludes direct contact between the foreign trader and the end user of the product. Hence, the initial contact with the Chinese is likely to be indirect. You are approached by or approach somebody acting for another party (who still need not be the end user of your product or, if you are buying, the supplier).

The Chinese bureaucracy

If the deal originates in China the process that the Chinese must go through before you are approached is complex as well as methodical. The local plant or industry committee perceives a need for, say, machinery of a special kind. They will initiate discussions with the State Planning Commission, which may consider acquiring the machinery from overseas. If so, it must pass the request through a procedure aimed at carefully scrutinizing the merits of the case for overseas acquisition. (The potential benefits of China acquiring a new technology play a role here.)

If the proposal survives this process (and, in view of the shortages of foreign exchange, it will compete with others under consideration at that time), the Ministry of Foreign Trade will seek, through its overseas agencies, information on potential sellers of the machinery. It could invite overseas suppliers to address technical seminars in China (these might be your first contact with the Chinese as potential customers). There is, however, still a long way to go before the potential order for your products is turned into an actual order for delivery of the goods, and you ought not to count your chickens yet, or indeed even think about them!

The two-stage negotiating process, familiar to traders with the Soviets, will be followed. One set of negotiations will take place on the technical aspects of the product, usually with somebody representing the end user. Another set of negotiations will get under way regarding the commercial aspects of the deal, usually with representatives of the ministry financing the exchange.

Even assuming that everything goes reasonably well in the often prolonged negotiations, the actual decision to initiate the purchase must still await bureaucratic approval from those whose task it is to operate and implement the state plans. What suits the Chinese agency that you have dealt with, let alone what suits you, does not necessarily carry the same weight with those whose horizons are bounded by other weighty matters, such as fitting the pressing demand for goods into an already elaborately conceived plan that must, on paper at least, balance requirements against resources.

Imports and exports in China are constrained by the country's overall economic guidelines, which include the availability of foreign currency to pay for imports. The Ministry of Foreign Trade is charged with the responsibility for meeting import and export targets and is extremely reluctant to adapt its policies to meet new demands without prolonged consultation with all the overlapping bureaucratic interests who have or are likely to have an opinion about the decision or its implications.

There is no doubt that the Chinese bureaucracy is as cumbersome and as slow as any found in Communist regimes. Its follies are partly based on the interests of self-preservation of the individual bureaucrats and partly on the functional interests of the system.

If a monopoly of foreign trade is dictated by the interests of preserving a Communist economic and social system, then it behooves those charged with implementing the policy to exercise their monopolistic powers in the time-honored way of all bureaucracies: with due care and attention to detail. In a word, slowly.

And you can take it that Chinese bureaucrats do precisely this. They are not too worried about the inevitable delay this causes before they are in a position to make a decision to open negotiations with you (which will be followed by further delays while they get confirmation of the negotiated deal you have agreed to with them).

Making the first approach

Since China is a heavily centralized society, the Chinese that you deal with will more than likely be based in Peking, and it is in this ancient city that you will do most of your negotiating. Getting there in a physical sense is much easier than getting an invitation to go there.

You could try the unsolicited approach if you don't mind having to put up with being a "tourist" rather than a business negotiator (and what better city to be a tourist in than Peking?), but on the whole an unsolicited trip, assuming that the Chinese grant you a visa for one, is likely to be a waste of your (business) time. You are almost certainly never going to be able to sort out who to see, where to find them, and what influence they have on an uninvited trip of this nature.

Probably the best approach is to make contact with the relevant commercial section of the nearest Chinese embassy to you. Please, make sure that you know the difference between the People's Republic of China and the Republic of China; otherwise, you could end up by asking for a visa to Taiwan China instead of Peking China and believe me, there is a difference!

You can offer them samples of your business literature, including detailed technical descriptions of your products. They will, in due course, forward these to the relevant ministry in Peking. If you know which ministry covers your products, or which foreign trade corporation is responsible for importing them, you can, of course, send your technical literature directly to them in China.

Whichever approach you use, you would be best advised not to expect an early reaction. By "early" I mean a response in anything much less than a year. This is your first lesson in patience and you should learn it well. There will be many more before you actually receive your first check from the Bank of China!

Other ways of getting your products to the notice of Chinese negotiators include attendance at trade fairs in China or, if you belong to an appropriate organization, through visiting China as a member of a delegation (perhaps sponsored by your trade association or the U.S. government).

You can also arrange, at your own company's expense, to hold a technical seminar in Peking and, through this, demonstrate your products and your technical competence to interested Chinese bureaucrats. In fact, their first response to your approach might very well be to offer you such a facility, with you bearing your own costs and them in return rounding up myriads of their specialists to sit in on your demonstrations and talks.

If the Chinese approach you first—perhaps your product has come to their attention in a technical journal—you are obviously a little further down the negotiating track than if you make the first move, although I would not base your export program to China on the expectation of them coming to you.

Technical negotiations

No matter how far down the track you start you will still need to go through the serious business of technical evaluation of your product. You should remember, while this is going on, that these meetings are a part of, not separate from, the negotiation.

The technical negotiations can be exhausting, and the more that you tire of them the more likely you will be to make concessions in a vain attempt to speed them up ("a decision, give me a decision, anything for a decision!").

HOW MUCH FOR ONE?

China does not have an indigenous civil aviation industry, and in the 1960s purchased civil aircraft from both Britain (Tridents) and the United States (Boeings). These negotiations were long and arduous since the Chinese fought over every clause and for every cent.

Having got the aircraft delivered and in operation, they discovered that they did not have the equipment to move the aircraft around the runways and that only one firm in the world supplied the necessary vehicles.

As the Chinese, for a change, were in a hurry, they telexed this U.S. firm and asked them to quote a price for one of their vehicles. The firm replied by telex with a price quote.

The next telex they received asked them to quote for twenty vehicles and demanded a quantity discount!

The U.S. firm replied with a discounted price and received an order for delivery immediately.

The Chinese might have got a bigger discount if they had got a discounted price for ten vehicles in the first instance, followed by twenty, but even so they did all right as instant purchasers in the U.S. market.

Your response to a technical interrogation (and it could last for thirty or forty working days) ought to be a combination of great patience, respect for your Chinese opponents, and an absolute determination to be prepared to bring the technical discussions to an end when clearly they are using them for improper (in the commercial sense) purposes.

The absent end user

You may try, if you wish, to counterinterrogate the Chinese on the end user of your product. You are unlikely to be offered much in the way of information about who will use your product, what they will use it for, and what conditions they will use it under. This makes it a trifle difficult to adjust your proposition to the needs of the user, which could be important in relation to the specifications that you agree to and the arrangements you make regarding maintenance, servicing, training, and spare parts to be included in the deal.

It is easier to move mountains with one's bare hands than it is to get the Chinese to tell you much about the end user. They live in a highly secretive society, distinctly compartmentalized, and operate under a "need to know" policy among themselves that could be a model for a paranoid security organization.

Their unwillingness to discuss the end user might also be due to the simple fact that they do not know the answers to your questions themselves. Evidence suggests, though, that even if they do know the answers they regard them as none of your business and cannot see why or how this limits your ability to provide them with tailor-made service.

Commercial negotiations

Once the commercial stage of the negotiations is entered, the Chinese will press for concessions on everything from price per unit through financing for the deal to delivery and the usual panoply of penalty clauses. Given that the technical aspects of the deal are dealt with first, it is reasonable to withhold commitments on prices and financing until this stage is complete. (Watch those commitments they want from you to include training their personnel in the package without charge.)

In your eagerness to enter the Chinese market you might signal—even in writing!—price concessions from the start. If you do, you will regret your haste with even greater speed once they start talking about money.

The outlook of the Chinese buyer is clouded by his perceptions of your company as a member of the capitalist system, with you in the unlikely role of a bourgeois exploiter, ruthlessly playing the market to get fabulous and unjustified profits. He also knows that you live in a competitive environment—alien to his experience of living under a state monopoly—and believes that his monopoly position representing the "workers and peasants of China" enables him to put competitive pressure on you.

Not having much competition available internally to push you on price, the Chinese will quote external competition, perhaps from within your own country. They are quite prepared to stage-manage some "capitalist" competition, or expose you to signs of some real competition that happens to be in town, in order to put elementary price pressure on you.

Now, it is amazing, given the facts of life in capitalist societies where competition is a daily experience, that many American negotiators price-crumble with alarming speed (not to say alacrity) when faced with price pressure from Communist negotiators. Naturally, such behavior only encourages the Chinese to repeat the same demands to every visiting U.S. negotiator, since it appears to be a successful way to provoke bouts of price-crumbling.

If American negotiators selling valuable products in China

see this market as one in which they must cut to the bone and beyond in the matter of prices, it little behooves the Chinese to teach them their business. The vulnerability of suppliers to versions of the "sell cheap, get famous" gambit is legendary in U.S. economies, but many who should know better seem totally helpless when the guy trying it is wearing a Mao suit and appears to be representing one billion potential customers. The fact that going in with very low prices does not lead to massive future business ought to be a sufficient caution to you if you are ever tempted by the illusion that it will.

The use of competition

In the West most of us have heard of the "Dutch auction" technique of selling. Briefly, in a Dutch auction the price to be paid for an item is reduced successively until somebody calls out that he or she will buy it at that price. Naturally, the pressure is on the bidders, because whoever calls out first gets the item at whatever price the auctioneer has reached. They can remain silent and hope that nobody will call out at the last bid, thus forcing the auctioneer to try a lower price. If they get it wrong and a rival bids at the going price, those who remained silent are automatically shut out of the bidding.

(The standard U.S. auction reverses this procedure. The auctioneer calls out successively higher bids, and bidders signal their willingness to pay that price. When there is nobody else bidding the last bidder gets the item at whatever price the auctioneer last called.)

The Chinese often play off rivals for their business in a version of a Dutch auction. They will take your price offers as they are presented and disclose them to your rivals, who may even be in the next room. (I heard of one negotiation in Canton where the rivals were seated at adjacent tables and able to hear directly what each said as the Chinese negotiators moved openly between them!)

Your rival has the opportunity to match or better your offer. If you find this reprehensible, remember you will almost certainly be given the opportunity to respond to your rival's bids. It is a test of your nerve not to be drawn into such a game. The general effect is, of course, that U.S. negotiators have their prices forced down, sometimes below the point of profitability.

You will be told by the Chinese negotiator that you face lots of competition. They may not overtly believe in free competition for ideological reasons, but do not let that fool you: They think they know how to make competition work in the national interests of China. This generally consists of acting the part of the aggressive buyer waiting for you and your rivals to maul each other's prices.

For obvious reasons, you are a long way from home when you are negotiating in Peking. You are likely to have spent some considerable time in negotiations before you reach the question of price. By pressuring you into believing that everyone and his uncle are in the next room ready to sign the deal you have spent months trying to put together, the Chinese hope you will crumble and give the goods to them even cheaper, rather than pack your bags and go home empty-handed.

The remedy is in your hands. Don't price-crumble because they tell you about, or even show you in the flesh, the competition. Tie your deal together with conditional propositions; link every element of it to others to prevent them from picking off concessions on an item-by-item basis; and, above all, insist that if they alter the terms of one item in the deal you must make a corresponding adjustment in another item. If you do not apply some version of this advice you will end up being Dutch-auctioned into numerous concessions.

THE SHIFTING CHINESE MIDDLE

An American corporation, world-renowned in the oil industry, was asked by the Chinese to enter into negotiations to
supply services to the small but growing domestic Chinese
off-shore oil industry.

The Chinese, who are anxious to develop their oil resources
and use U.S. technology to do so, went hard at the prices
quoted by the American team.

First, they got a price quotation for the U.S. company to
supply its services for three years, then they demanded inclu-
sive of the quoted price a lot of extras.

Among these extras were some very expensive add-ons,
such as free training for Chinese nationals, free manuals for
operating the specialized equipment, masses of spares and
supplies, and domestic charges for accommodating the company's technical staff. This last was a trifle ambitious on the
part of the Chinese—they insisted that foreign staff be
charged at the same per diem rate for subsistence that the
Chinese were charged for their staff visiting the United
States, where prices and living standards are, of course, much
higher.

The U.S. negotiators fought hard to avoid pricing themselves into unprofitability and regularly complained that
when they made a concession the result was not a reciprocal
move on the part of the Chinese. Far from it. The Chinese regarded "split the difference" moves as invitations to put
pressure on the Americans to move even closer to the Chinese
opening position.

The remedy to a similar situation is in your hands: Pad your
prices before you open negotiations; never make a single concession without getting something back from the Chinese;
avoid any "fair play" illusions about split the difference gambits; totally resist the add-on ploys; and, lastly, sit it out, because the Chinese need oil technology (and much else
besides) far more than U.S. corporations need to work in
China.

Pad your prices

Another way to protect your prices is to anticipate price pressure from the start and to pad them beforehand. Failure to do this, in a misguided effort to look price-competitive against real and imaginary competition, can leave you short when you collect on your invoices.

You should bear in mind that the only reason that you are even talking to the Chinese about a potential deal is that they, or rather somebody in the labyrinthian Chinese bureaucracy, has decided that they need the type of product that you are so anxious to sell to them (or, if they are exporting, they need the earnings that they will get from selling their products to you).

This means that you are not in a casual or opportunistic negotiating relationship with the Chinese. If you see them across the table from you, you can take it that somebody somewhere in their country wants to do business with you if you can supply them with what they are ordered to acquire.

Anticipating price pressure is particularly important in the matter of the negotiations on how the deal is to be financed. "Who gets how much of the money and when do they get it?" is not an idle question. They may be Communists dedicated to the proposition that capitalist finance is robbery, but they sure know how to squeeze careless capitalists who forget to cover themselves against financial payment routines designed to provide Chinese customers with free credit.

Letters of credit

The Chinese pay for their exports and imports using the letter of credit system. The demand for foreign currency is so high in the spending plans of the Chinese foreign trade corporations that they cannot pay for everything they wish to purchase by means of foreign (hard) currency reserves. Hence, they use the letter of credit system to ease their foreign exchange problems at the expense of foreign traders who make unwarranted assumptions about when cash and goods are supposed to change hands.

The Chinese operate their foreign trade using contracts that they have drawn up beforehand, and they rigidly refuse to allow amendments to these preprinted contracts, especially when the amendments are designed to suit the interests of the foreign trader.

When they are exporting Chinese produce they require that the foreign purchaser open a "confirmed, irrevocable, transferable and divisible" letter of credit in favor of the seller (i.e., China) at a branch or approved agent of the Bank of China. The phraseology is important. The fact that the letter of credit is *confirmed* means that the importer's bank guarantees payment as long as the documentation meets the terms of the contract; it is *irrevocable* in order to prevent an importer withholding payment for any reason whatsoever, including the condition of the goods when they arrive (a singularly blanket condition which the Chinese do not reciprocate with respect to their own imports); it is *transferable* to enable the Bank of China to use it directly to pay for other transactions; and it is *divisible* to give flexibility in using it for part-payments.

The letter of credit comes into operation up to thirty days before the Chinese agency is due to ship the goods *toward* the importer. In some cases this could literally mean the exworks shipment date and not the sailing date at the Chinese port. If the actual date of shipment is delayed (and delays of some months are not unknown in China), this all means effectively that the importer has paid for the goods before getting sight of them. It also means he has unwittingly gotten into the lending money at no charge business, which is a surefire way to go bankrupt.

The only thing that the importer might have caught sight of is the draft on his bank requiring it to pay to the Bank of China the full import price of the goods. You can see why you have to be careful here in accepting stringent terms in the letter of credit! If you don't, you had better take a crash course in banking. Your credit control people might have views about your negotiating skills if you accept contract terms that turn you into an international moneylender instead of an importer of soy sauce.

Having lent the Chinese government considerable sums of money, no doubt you will come to be regarded by the Chinese as a great friend of China. If you are rich enough to afford this privilege, good luck to you. If you aren't, then you had better build into your purchase prices some amount to cover the interest you are effectively having to forgo to permit them to borrow from you. From the Chinese point of view, the use of free credit of this nature enables them to use your money to finance their other transactions, and it is a good business for them to be in. With annual exports worth over 500 million dollars, the savings in interest they create by using free credit is quite considerable.

When it comes to imports into China a similar letter of credit system operates, and it has the same characteristic of being designed to benefit the People's Republic of China rather than the supplier. China makes its payments for its imports by letters of credit issued to suppliers that are payable only at the Bank of China (thus curtailing separate trading in Chinese letters of credit in international markets). These letters of credit are also irrevocable, transferable and divisible, though they are not confirmed. This has the effect of enabling the Bank of China to withhold payments from you in certain cases. Neither are they truly irrevocable as described under exports: all imports into China are subject to their state inspection, and payment is only authorized when imports meet Chinese government standards and their interpretation of the contract.

To get payment after a shipment has been dispatched you will have to send your documents of proof to Peking. From this moment on you have no control over the transaction, since you have let your products and the original documents for payment out of your sight. Your commercial interests are now truly at the mercy of the People's Republic of China.

It can take time to get your payments processed at the Bank of China in Peking. Every day's delay is an interest-free loan to the Chinese government. If you try to circumvent this by getting a bank in your own country to pay you on account while the Bank of China wades through its own procedures, it will cost you what the local bank charges for discounting your invoices. You ought, therefore, to reflect your generosity as a lender of currency to the Chinese or your costs as a discountee to your local bank in your pricing policies. In other words, your prices must reflect the true costs to you of doing business with the Chinese; otherwise you will end up too poor to do business with them or anyone.

Contract negotiations

The crunch is going to come when you are negotiating the commercial contract. The Chinese share with the Japanese an aversion to legalistic language, particularly where it is confusing or obscure. They do not share the Japanese aversion to detail in their contracts, following in this respect a more Stalinist model of contract design. One contract with China worth 125 million dollars had a page in it for every million, and it covered every conceivable eventuality. It, like most other Chinese contracts, was unashamedly biased in favor of them rather than the supplier.

If you can get a straightforward sales or purchase contract without complications and conditions, you can consider yourself very lucky. Under such a contract you get paid or pay when the goods are shipped (subject to whatever concessions they have squeezed out of you regarding financing through their letters of credit).

Barter trade

China, like the USSR and other soft-currency countries, has expanded the role of barter in its international trading, and earlier remarks on this subject apply.

China trades with 167 countries and has over 80 bilateral trading agreements in operation. Some proportion of this trade can be paid for in hard currency earnings, some through extended credit deals with Western banks. Both means of payment have constraints. Hard foreign currency has to be earned, normally from hard-currency countries. It is not always the case that the recipients of China's trade have sufficient foreign currency holdings themselves (for example, Third World clients are short of hard currency too). With extended credit from world banks, the obvious problem is the debt-servicing requirements which can alarm a developing country faced with massive and growing overseas borrowings.

Barter trade can be attractive in these circumstances. China can contract to use its abundant and relatively cheap labor to process, or part-process, raw materials supplied by foreign traders and to re-export them to the supplier for worldwide distribution. The supplier might even supply the machinery too, and China could receive its fees for doing this in the form of some proportion of the output of the plant.

This system can enable the Chinese to acquire machinery and equipment not otherwise available to them. It is to be

CHINESE BARTER DEALS

The Chinese have gone into bartering in a big way, largely because their foreign trade requirements have expanded faster than their ability to finance them with hard-currency earnings.

Some barter transactions have been a trifle bizarre, such as when an Australian company in 1979 traded six 200-room prefabricated hotels for large quantities of frozen and canned food!

Most deals tend to be related in some way. For instance, for setting up shrimp farms the supplier gets paid in supplies of shrimp. Similar deals occur with oil pipelines' being paid for with supplies of oil, chemical plants with chemical output, light bulb plants with supplies of light bulbs, television plants with television sets, shipping container plants with shipping containers, and so on.

expected that when the Chinese territories adjacent to Hong Kong are in full operation as manufacturing and processing areas, this form of barter contract will become even more significant.

It takes time

In summary, negotiating with the Chinese authorities is bound to entail considerable time commitments on the part of U.S. companies, and they will follow the Soviet two-stage model of technical negotiations first, followed by commercial negotiations afterwards.

You will deal with one of the foreign trade corporations acting on behalf of the end user in respect to the product and on behalf of the finance ministry in respect to the financing

TIPS FOR TRAVELERS IN CHINA

Chinese people have conflicting attitudes to things foreign. They know that they need foreigners to help them develop economically, and at the same time they resent this dependence as an affront to China's dignity. Be prepared for bouts of xenophobia, followed by incredible and touching displays of kindness.

In 1979 China adopted its own version of a romanized script for its characters. Out went "Peking" and in came "Beijing," Canton became Guangzhou, Mao Tse-tung became Mao Zedong, and so on. It is customary to use the local name when abroad, though permissible to use American versions when at home. In Peking *always* refer to Beijing, and only refer to Mao if your hosts mention him (he may be in or out of political favor at the time). Avoid the Great Leap Forward, the Cultural Revolution, Madame Mao, and Taiwan.

It's cold in Peking from November to March, so dress accordingly. In Shanghai and Canton it's generally warm. Central heating and air conditioning are not common anywhere, hence dress warmer or cooler than you would if you were visiting Japan or moving around the United States.

Chinese businesses work from 8 A.M. to 6 P.M. six days a week. You get Sundays off, though shops are open every day. Visitors can shop in "Friendship Stores," which carry limited quantities of imports.

Hotel accommodation is scarce. Your hosts will arrange rooms or suites for you. Do not expect advance warning of where you are staying. Guest houses are an alternative if you are part of a large party, but make sure meals are included. If you book a taxi (you cannot hail one in the street), keep it for the day. Once you give it up you may never see it again!

Do not tip anyone with cash. It's illegal. Discreet gifts to the hotel for distribution to staff are acceptable. Do not make any sexual advances to anybody—the Chinese are very prudish.

Be ready for regular toasts during a meal. Always reciprocate. "To the friendship of our peoples" is a good standby, if you get stuck.

Do not take photographs that include airfields, bridges, docks, public buildings in them. Also avoid cute children and elderly people as subjects unless you ask them first.

Everything you take into China must be accounted for before you leave. All Chinese money must be left behind.

for the deal. The composition of the Chinese negotiating teams will vary depending on the subject under discussion, and most of the time your opposite number will not have authority to make a settlement without consultation upwards into the Chinese bureaucracy.

The Chinese will need time to consider whether to import your product in its entirety or to import those parts of it that they cannot manufacture themselves (this matter is important when the subject of spare parts is being discussed).

Their financial interests are influenced by their shortage of foreign currency, and they will therefore be likely to attempt to finance the deal using the letter of credit system. The pitfalls in this system from your point of view are summed up in the warning that you may unwittingly and unintentionally end up a lender to the Chinese government. The guy sitting next to you on the flight to Peking could be financing your deal through his badly negotiated letter of credit; conversely, you may be about to negotiate a deal that gives the Chinese sufficient free credit to pay for his deal.

The Chinese appear to be awakening to the vast opportunities for trade with the rest of the world, and they have abandoned the fallacy that they can "leap forward" from relative economic backwardness to prosperity entirely by themselves. But they have a long way to go and could very easily falter or be forced to retreat, depending on the politics of the leadership of the Communist party.

If you have something to sell them that they want badly enough to talk to you at all, you ought to bear this in mind when they try well-established "capitalist" ploys to frighten you into giving them your products at give-away prices. You can bet yourself a bowl of fried rice to a chicken chop suey that though they are (presently?) of a communistic disposition they can teach a lot of capitalistic managers a thing or two about commercial negotiating.

If you have any doubts on this score you should consider just how good the overseas Chinese are at doing business as fully fledged capitalists. You can take it from me that the Chinese still in China have not lost their touch when it comes to haggling!

ANSWERS TO SELF-ASSESSMENT TEST 7

1 a You are risking a heavy price squeeze which will put your profits under pressure or even eliminate them.   **(−10)**
b No! Never go for the sell cheap, get famous ploy. The Chinese use your hope of getting into their large potential market as a lever to force your prices down, but remember that the Chinese market is only a potential one and not yet a reality (China is a very poor country). Anyway, they have no intention of becoming dependent on the United States for key resources, such as engineering products. **(−15)**
c This is much the best move. Always pad your prices when opening negotiations in a new and untried market. The Chinese will expect you to do so and will be very disappointed, to the point of disbelief, if you try to hold your prices in the face of demands for discounts. **(10)**

2 a You are optimistic if you think they will allow their goods out of their sight without payment from you in their hands. To do this exposes them to the entire risk of the transaction, and anyway they need the money sooner rather than later.   **(−10)**

b Logic and fair play say yes, but practice is different. Those responsible for dispatching the goods are not the same as those responsible for receiving the money, and the latter guys are very cautious about risks. **(−5)**

c Yes. Chinese sales contracts specify a payment date of up to thirty days before the dispatch date. Bear in mind that the Chinese version of a dispatch date is usually in the form of "November–December 1986" and not a specific day in the year. You would therefore (in this example) pay for the goods on October 1, 1986 and could receive them at any time up to, say, February 1987, allowing for the sailing time and the usual delays. **(10)**

3 a No! You are clearly an honorable trader, but the Chinese do not see things your way. While you as an importer will be required to open an irrevocable letter of credit in their favor (see question 2), you will not be permitted by its terms to revoke payment for any reason whatsoever; however, their obligation to pay you by an irrevocable credit for your exports to them is qualified by their right to inspect the goods on arrival in China. They can do this because they put all their transactions through the state Bank of China, and they hold all the aces when it comes to payments. **(−10)**

b You will not be caught napping in China—though I doubt whether you will be able to avoid the usual risks of doing business with them. Some consolation: The Chinese are very good at paying what they agree to when they agree to do so; there are very few cases of disputes and even fewer of default. **(10)**

SELF-ASSESSMENT TEST 8

1 You are selling highly specialized steels to a German company which agrees to proceed to contract, but just before signing they tell you that they must get a 10 percent price cut if the order is to go ahead. Do you:

a Say no?
b Say yes?
c Agree if, and only if, your prices are free on board (FOB) instead of cost, insurance and freight (CIF)?

2 You discover accidentally that your Swedish customer has been marking up your products by 800 percent while squeezing your prices under the threat of stiff competition from your rivals. Do you:

a Confront them with what you have discovered and demand a price increase?
b Save your information until the next price negotiation?
c Ask them casually for details of their local pricing policy without disclosing what you know?
d Say nothing because what they pay you is profitable anyway?

3 You are negotiating to buy a propulsion system from a British manufacturer. What is likely to be the most difficult thing to agree upon?

a Price
b Financing
c Delivery
d Quality

CHAPTER 8

The European Tribes—or, Negotiating with People Divided by a Common Future

Old enmities

Europeans do a lot of business with each other. They used to spend a lot of time fighting, thinking about fighting, or resting between fights. Apart from the bloodshed, little has changed. Now they fight over beef, lamb, and fish quotas, imports, taxes, grants, funds, and economic policies. Those who thought that the European Economic Community (EEC) was going to change the nature of the European peoples quickly obviously got it all wrong. The EEC hasn't changed them at all—at least not yet; it has only given their eternal conflicts a new dimension.

Not that this is something to complain about. Better that Germany and Britain argue over a couple of dozen cheap flights for civil passengers between their cities than that their talented peoples spend hours planning to send bombers over their respective populations; better that France is flooded with cheap Italian wine than that Italy is overrun by the descendants of Napoleon.

The history of Europe clearly has deeply influenced the relationships between all of its peoples. Though the last European war (called Hitler's war nowadays, as if the rest of Europe wished to disavow shared responsibility for it) ended forty years ago, it still influences the attitudes of ordinary people, if less so the attitudes of the young (always defined as anybody less than half our own age).

Old enmities die hard but there is hope. The popular British press loves to "hate" the French for their insistence on arranging European affairs to suit French national interests. If the normally staid British can switch sides so dramatically—assuming this is not just another manifestation of European intertribal warfare, with allies and enemies switching roles at the drop of a franc or a deutschemark—it suggests, perhaps, that the enmities are not too serious.

Within Britain they take their enmities more seriously. I know people called MacDonald who still will not speak to a Campbell or enter a place of business owned by a Campbell, and it makes not one whit of difference whether they know or need them or not, so deep is the massacre of MacDonalds by Campbells at Glencoe in 1692 engrained in MacDonald folklore.

In Northern Ireland, the Irish of the two communities continue to fight out their ancient enmities with a ferocity totally beyond the understanding of outsiders. One side marches to tunes praising King "Billy" of 1690 while the other has memories of martyrs and massacres going back to Cromwell's time.

The rivalry between England and Scotland is a somewhat less serious business, largely confined to the exertions of twenty-two men on a soccer field once a year.

From the Atlantic to the Urals

Europe is a divided land. Geographically, according to the great French patriot Charles de Gaulle, it stretches variously from the Atlantic to the Urals and from beyond the Arctic Circle to the Mediterranean. Politically it is divided into East and West by the Iron Curtain. It is also divided into North and South by the weather—rain, snow, cold winds, and odd spells of sunshine to the north; sunshine, hot climes, and occasional rain to the south.

It is, or rather could be, the world's largest economic power, though its very real divisions preclude such an eventuality in the near future. If it was a united federation of states it would certainly be the dominant force in the world in almost all spheres, political, economic, technological, and military.

The division of Europe into separate states, each with a national language and all the other trappings of statehood, is the great fact that must be faced, with all its complexity and consequences. It is the divisions that determine the business culture (as much as all other kinds of culture), and it is these that negotiators must come to terms with when contemplating engaging in trade with Europe. Trade within Europe is rapidly growing, as it was meant to do under the EEC, and there is no sign that intra-European trade is anywhere near saturation point. So, if you are in the international trade business at all, it is more than likely that you will be negotiating in one or more of the European states before long.

There is a considerable range of business behavior in Europe, much of it conforming to national stereotypes, though you must be careful to allow for changing trends and tastes since the integrative influences of increasing trade and contact between the nations are clearly wearing down national distinctions. Particularly with the influence of mass culture (or, to be frank, the modern pop culture of the post-war generations), the safe stereotypes are looking more fragile than most people thirty or forty years ago would have thought likely. Especially among the youth it is more difficult to tell one nationality from another until they start speaking.

Nevertheless the distinctions, if a trifle blurred, are still recognizable, and you will not go too far wrong by paying them some attention; at the worst, you will appear a little dated when you act as if they still exist in their full flower and glory.

The Germans

We can begin with the Germans. They represent the modern Europe in two distinct ways: first, they are divided into East and West by the very real border that separates the Federal Republic of Germany of the West from the German Democratic Republic (GDR) of the East; second, each zone has the highest living standard and most advanced economy of its respective allies. Please note, however, that people in the GDR do not like to hear their country referred to as "East Germany" or their government as the East German regime.

For the purposes of this chapter, following common usage, I shall refer to the Federal German Republic as Germany. While much of what is said about Germany can also be applied to the GDR, you ought to bear in mind that the Communist economic and political system in the GDR qualifies the actual operation of its business culture, Germanic as the GDR may be overall. (I was once told by a Polish Communist that the reason the East Germans were so successful had more to do with the fact that they were Germans than the fact that they were Communists.)

The Germans have a well-deserved reputation for efficiency. They are capable of immense technical ingenuity and are extremely persistent in pursuit of their goals. Their industries operate to exacting technical standards, and they expect the highest quality in the products that they buy or sell. If you are going to do business with the Germans you will have to convince them that your company can meet consistent standards in all aspects of the deal, and to some extent the way that they perceive your performance in the negotiations will be determined by how convincing you are about meeting your commitments in this respect.

They certainly will approach the negotiations with a thoroughly professional preparation. This will extend not just to the product that you have come to buy or sell; it will also include thorough research on your company as a potential business partner. They will want to know, for example, just how financially sound your company is and how your proposition reflects that soundness. In financial matters they are extremely conservative and are risk-averse, so you should be ready to answer very detailed questions about your company as well as your proposals.

In their own business affairs they have relied on their banks for much of their finance (unlike the British they do not rely on a securities market to raise business financing). Since banks the world over are bastions of caution and timidity, you will find the Germans ultracautious about propositions that leave them exposed to more than a modest risk of losses.

Germany functions because of its economic strength—a sound currency (which constitutionally is under the control of the Federal Bank, not the government) is one manifestation of its strength, a highly productive workforce is another—and this strength is not based on highly opportunistic investments. The Germans invest in sound projects, using sound finance, with sound prospects of getting a profitable return. They choose to work with companies abroad only if they have something to offer that cannot be acquired locally and if they are unlikely to jeopardize German commercial strengths.

The German preference for local purchases is thus not purely nationalistic (as it is in France, for example). The integrity of a local company is more susceptible to close scrutiny than that of an overseas company. A German company has a local reputation, and if it passes the usual tests it is more likely to get the business than a company outside Germany. But Germany does not have a monopoly in all aspects of technology and all products. They will buy from a foreigner if the foreigner has technological or other advantages that cannot be found in Germany and if the foreigner can deliver the products at the high standards the Germans require.

So you can expect to be given a hard time when proving to them that your company's products meet their requirements. Do not, however, assume that you can easily exploit the scarcity value of your unique product in the face of a clear wish of the Germans to acquire it. They may very well be anxious to buy your product, but you would not think so from the way they set about negotiating the commercial side of the deal.

The Germans are very good at commercial negotiating. They seem to be able to squeeze concessions out of nowhere once they decide to buy. It is not uncommon for the German negotiators to try for a last-minute discount before signing a contract—"It's a deal but you must come down 10 percent in price"—so you had better be ready for this. Either say no, or hold something back as a closing concession.

They will put pressure on your delivery dates, especially if you are supplying from a U.S. subsidiary in Britain (which is notorious all over Europe for lack of performance when it comes to delivery), arguing that they have to be assured of strict adherence to delivery promises to meet their own highly disciplined production schedules. You could find yourself agreeing to a tight penalty clause on top of an even tighter delivery schedule to get the business. To cover themselves they may even demand a generous (to them) warranty period for the performance of your product, plus extensive credit in anticipated compensation for your failing to meet them on this.

In fact, given the pleasant nature of the surroundings

where you are likely to be negotiating—such as a lovely room with a panoramic view across green fields—you might find yourself agreeing to all kinds of things. Much of German industry was rebuilt after the war in modern buildings (inside and out), usually in pleasant surroundings, particularly in Bavaria. There are lots of worse places on earth to visit each year to renegotiate your deals!

Germans are hard bargainers, not so much because they are hard people on a personal level, but because they are so well prepared and serious about their work. No matter how well you are established in your own country, it is likely that they will ask you for business references and where possible, for a demonstration of your product in action, either in your own plant or preferably in the plant of a current customer. They will want to talk to your technical people and to your customers, and all this before they get to the subject of price. Hence, you cannot be in too much of a hurry in the preliminaries to the deal.

Germany is a competitive environment to do business in, and the negotiators will use this fact to put pressure on your prices (they regularly mention the potential competition, just in case you forget it). Since they are doing business with you because they cannot get your product locally (at present), they will use the prospect of local competition to challenge your commercial proposals. The competition is real, and your presence in the market could be temporary. When combined, these factors will cause you to draw on depths of resolve not to crumble.

To get into the German market you will have to be good at whatever it is that you do, and to stay in the market you will have to stay ahead in a technical sense. Above all, you must reach and maintain high quality standards. Otherwise, you will find your technology being acquired and improved upon by a rival who speaks the same language as your current German customer.

In their personal relations German negotiators are formal, and they expect you to be also. Until or unless you know your German opposite number very well, you should always refer to him as "Herr Schmidt" (or as "Doktor Schmidt," if appropriate) rather than "Fritz," or, of course, "Frau Schmidt" unless she is under twenty. Formality extends to dress too, so get used to wearing a suit at almost all times. (Jeans are out, unless you are selling to the "alternative" youth society, in which case make sure that you do cash-only deals!) Whatever you wear, don't keep your hands in your pockets as it's regarded as rude.

The German disgust (there is no other word for it) at unreliability in the matter of deliveries is likely to be frostily brought to the surface if you are late for a business appointment. So get there on time, and remember they start work earlier than is usual in the United States—before 8 A.M.—and often finish later—around 8 P.M.

The one thing you won't have to worry about is getting paid, provided you meet the terms of your contract. Conversely, they don't like to be kept waiting for their money. Germans are punctilious in their business affairs, formal in their relationships, and genuinely competitive in their outlook.

The French

The French have the reputation of being the most highly patriotic people in Europe, but this could be misleading. The French government is extremely patriotic, since it is its job to represent the best interests of France in all matters, and business organizations tend to operate in the same way. But not all French citizens are as deeply attached to the centralized French state as the organizations you are likely to be doing business with, and it is therefore sensible to refrain from making assumptions about the nationalistic attitudes of those you negotiate with until you are sure that you are not dealing with a disaffected Breton, a southerner, or a Corsican.

It is true, however, that the French state works for France. It does not operate on behalf of foreigners, and if you come into contact with its representatives you should try not to behave as if you think its officials should pay special attention to your interests. (This is particularly true when dealing with policemen, customs officials, government clerks, and politicians.)

If you negotiate with the French it is more than likely that the negotiations will take place in the French language, even if the French negotiator speaks perfect English. They seldom make any concessions on this, unless they happen to be abroad and need your business badly. So if a French negotiator speaks to you in English you have probably received the biggest concession you are likely to get that day.

They are distant rather than formal, though they have a habit of shaking hands more times than you expect to wash your hands in a day. I have been introduced to the members of a French company's staff—all twenty-eight of them—with a handshake when I entered the room and received another one from each of them again when I left it. They do the same in cafés and bars.

It is always a good policy to turn up on time, no matter where you are in the world, but do not expect too much of the French in this respect. Sometimes they do and sometimes they don't, and they have a ready stock of plausible excuses—"the traffic" is the most common—for being late. If you are late, however, for any reason you will be received coolly, if they receive you at all, and they will still be waiting for you only if they need you (your second concession of the day?).

On social occasions, such as a formal dinner, there is an informal convention that the more important the chief guest

SIBERIAN GAS—WORST DEAL OF THE CENTURY?

Since 1984 Siberian natural gas has flowed 3600 miles to Western Europe, thanks to a 15-billion-dollar engineering feat of Western technology—and 10 billion dollars of European capital.

Nothing illustrates the politico-commercial skills of the Soviet Union better than the details of this deal. Their ability to have gotten highly talented Europeans to put up the capital and take most of the risks, and this for only about 20 percent of the gas (the rest being diverted to Soviet uses), is a remarkable testimony either to their negotiating prowess or to the negotiating errors of the Europeans.

How did the Soviets manage to pull off this coup? Simply by dividing the Germans, French, British, and Italians from each other. (They even managed to put one over on the Japanese, no mean feat.)

The Soviet negotiators went on tour from European company to European company, from German bank to French bank and then back again, each time picking up a concession here and a concession there. With their rivals making concessions, the Europeans responded with even greater concessions, to which inevitably the rivals responded too. Instead of treating this deal with a single monopolist customer as requiring a single European seller, the Western capitalist firms and their governments caved in one by one like lambs on their way to market.

The Dutch, with great credit to themselves, refused to play the Soviet game of Dutch auction and tried to get collaboration among the interested parties. The Soviet response was open and brutal—they cut the Dutch out of the deal and went on to tackle the rest on a one-by-one basis.

What was the deal? Basically, that the Western countries would finance the project, provide the necessary technology, and enter into purchase contracts at fixed prices for some of the gas.

The loans given to the Soviet Union were charged at a

below-market rate of 7 to 8 percent, with interest rates at the time running at 11 percent and over. The gas is to be purchased on twenty-five-year contracts at prices tied to a one-way oil price index (nice one, Ivan!). That is, if the world oil price index rises the Europeans pay more for their gas, but if it falls below a certain level they still pay a fixed minimum price ($5.70 per million Btu's, compared to Algerian gas prices at the time of writing of around $4.15), irrespective of how far the index falls. If oil prices fall from thirty-four dollars a barrel (the price when the deal was signed) to anything near twenty-four dollars a barrel, the German, French, and Italian consumers are going to look profligate in respect to the price their governments pay the Soviets for gas, and the Soviets are going to reap a windfall in hard currency.

The basic lesson is obvious. European negotiators must not deal with the Soviet Union separately on such massive joint projects. Their governments, concerned as they inevitably have to be with national unemployment, must not allow themselves to be persuaded to underwrite national companies that follow kamikaze price policies to get international business. Above all, the bottom line in any negotiation with the Soviet government must be that if the Soviets want to use European capital for their projects they will have to pay the market rate like everybody else does.

the later he or she will turn up. Therefore, if you are invited to a dinner with the company president you can expect him to arrive late, and hence you will start eating about thirty minutes after his due time. A cabinet minister will take at least fifty minutes to get there. Thus if you get hungry early eat with people of your own status, or eat something beforehand if you are invited to a function. Business meals almost certainly will be in a restaurant and seldom, if ever, in a person's house. I once made an awful mistake and called on a senior dealer at his luxurious apartment in Paris, having arrived early by plane. I was very quickly, though politely, shunted to a hotel and reminded that our meeting was fixed for 8 P.M. that evening. I'm sure that this killed the deal (though the meal was delicious).

Don't turn up late yourself. It won't impress anybody because in French social terms foreigners are not important enough to be excused lateness. If you are stuck waiting for someone in these circumstances do not mention your irritation, try to ignore the delay, and enter into general conversation with whoever has turned up on time. The French are passionate conversationalists and respect the same in others. (Do not drink while waiting, since you might be well oiled by the time the others arrive! If thirsty, drink mineral water.)

France dies in August. The entire nation is on holiday, and no business is possible. Paris is totally empty except for tourists, and the beaches in the South (many of them topless) are packed tight. The French love their vacations, and no number of inducements will persuade them to miss or delay one for a negotiation.

Even in the last week of July their minds are switched off from business, so you should avoid trying to squeeze a French visit into your schedule then. If you think that you have persuaded a French negotiator to take your proposal away with him on vacation and work on it for your later return, either you are the victim of a mild con or you and he are in the vacation campsite business and he is testing your products. Better leave your business deals until September.

The French have no compunction about taking advantage of you in a negotiation if they have the economic leverage to do so. They will hold you strictly to the deal and nothing but the deal for as long as it suits them. If it doesn't they will breach the deal and defy you to stop them.

Precedents exist for this odd behavior. The French government always acts in the national interest irrespective of what the EEC or anybody else says. If they don't want to receive Japanese exports they will introduce nontariff barriers of the most blatant kind, such as requiring each and every item to be individually inspected at an obscure customs hall in the middle of rural France. The informal (and illegal) hijacking of cheap Italian wine or British lamb imports is well known and more or less tolerated by the authorities and the police.

Hence, you must examine the contract carefully. If you make concessions to get the business and accept some of the penalties they will endeavor to introduce, then you know what you will be in for if circumstances arise to occasion the penalties. This can lead to acrimonious relationships, which will mainly feature the French sitting on their hands if they are in the wrong or suing you if they think you are.

Relationships with the French must be entered into on a long-term basis before you get the normality of goodwill common to relationships with others. If you can establish a good rapport with a French company over many years and can trade to mutual advantage without the blessing of accidental upsets, you will find them extremely compatible partners. They might even warm to you socially, and the payoff that follows in terms of good food, great wine, and lovely weather will make the atrocities of the past well worth enduring.

In addition, exposure to the company of men and women who dress extremely well will do wonders for your fashion sense. It's more than likely that your best business suit will look tired next to the clothes your French opposite number and his or her staff are wearing, so don't turn up for a meeting in your second-best clothes!

The Italians

If the French can be exasperating in the punctuality with which they sometimes attend formal dinners, the Italians are among the least punctual people in Europe. (The Arabs, however, deserve a place in the Guinness Book of Records for lack of punctuality, though some South Americans are even more lax.) That is assuming that they turn up at all. I learned the hard way to check beforehand by telephone whether a carefully arranged meeting was still scheduled—and even then on occasion found it had been unilaterally postponed during the time it took me to cross town by taxi!

Italian business leaders are extremely autocratic when it comes to dealing with subordinates within their own organizations and not much more democratic when dealing with outsiders. Their organizations relish protocol and status, and they never accept an insult lying down. They are, however, *always* extremely charming about everything they do, even when telling you no or when telling you something more direct to do with yourself.

The Italians have a volatile temperament. One minute they are as high as a kite and the next as low as a client for the Samaritans. They gesticulate wildly, their shoulders, arms, and hands convulsing in tempo with their voices. It can be a spectacle just to watch them making a point, preferably in good humor, because if they are angry the performance verges on hysteria. (If you see two Italians apparently about to come to blows do not intervene; they could just be arguing about whose turn it is to pay for the taxi.)

Italians love style; in fact they live by it. *Bella figura* is no small part of their view of the world. Business negotiators tend to dress smartly, groom themselves neatly, and occupy modern well-equipped offices. (A haircut in Italy is worth having even if you don't need one—it's complete with espresso served at your chair.) They make entrances and exits with a flourish, eat and drink well (but not excessively—so watch your drinking; water your booze down with *acqua minerale*), and talk about their families with pride. The Italian adult has infinite patience with children, and you can expect a restaurant to tolerate a degree of wildness in the children of diners bordering on license. If your business lunch is disturbed by kids running around do not get angry and under no circumstances chastise even the most boorish behavior by a child. Your Italian colleagues would be horrified if you showed irritation at what they regard as the natural behavior of children.

They are more informal than Germans and less distant than the French, though they are often impersonal in business matters. They take their time to make a decision, not, like the Chinese or Japanese, because they are consulting with colleagues, but out of a desire not to commit themselves too quickly. If you have a deadline or give them one for making a decision, they will go right up to it without batting an eyelid, such is their ability to play to the theater of a "crisis."

Government offices are closed in the afternoon, which can be inconvenient. The staff appear to moonlight with second and even third jobs, though the public scandal about this is likely to explode sooner or later. (It's also of interest to the tax authorities, as tax evasion is widespread.)

My brother-in-law is an Italian banker, and he keeps these half-day hours in common with the rest of his profession. He used to have a share in a family trattoria but since his promotion appears to have given this up, presumably for a more lucrative sideline. Like most Italian males he is very tight-lipped about his business deals, and he does not like being questioned about them. I only found out about the trattoria from my sister, and even she has gotten quiet about what her husband is up to!

The Mediterranean has an effect on all its peoples. Italians, like the Spaniards, love haggling, only more so. They will haggle all day if you let them, especially over prices (while Spaniards, and Greeks, do no business during afternoon siesta).

On other matters Italians are, strangely, less concerned, be it delivery, quality, or performance (though naturally they expect what they buy to work, and generally what they sell does). Whereas Germans will pay more in order to get the proper quality or delivery, Italians will try to pay less in a time-honored urge to save cash.

The country is measured along a north–south spectrum: the further south you are the less businesslike and commercial in a modern sense the people will be, except when it comes to haggling over food and accommodation. The north is the most industrialized part of the country and the closest to European norms of business conduct.

The south can be a nightmare for unescorted women. A great deal of male harassment (whistles, invitations, being followed, and so on) is inevitable, and local women can also be very rude, probably regarding you as a provocation to their menfolk. I've seen local women actually spit at unescorted foreign women sitting drinking in a restaurant. A woman hitching or offering a lift in a car on her own or even asking for directions will be assumed to be seeking a sexual liaison by many Italian males and will only escape, if this is not the intention, by the most firm use of the word no and appropriate gestures that are universally understood.

There are plenty of business opportunities in Italy for selling or buying components or finished products. If the products purchased are within their technology they will generally be of a high standard.

If Italians appear to be a little obsessed with their internal relationships and business contacts rather than with outsiders, this is because it is within those relationships that they find or seek their identity. Italy is a large inward-looking society, only half conscious of the world outside (as with the Dutch, nobody else speaks their language). While they are open to outsiders, they do not adapt their customs and outlooks for them; outsiders remain observers, not participants.

Italy remains very Italian—frantic, slightly inefficient, a

trifle disorganized, and in a hurry only to be late. It can be a rewarding place to do business in, providing you adjust to their culture and slow down to their tempo.

The Greeks

In Greece, a new member of the EEC (though its government has threatened to leave, which might just be its way of establishing a negotiating position), things are very Italian in tempo, only more so. The weather is hotter than in Italy, and most business negotiations will take place in Athens or nearby, which is, or appears to be, even warmer than the rest of the country. (It's certainly dirtier and smoggier.) So be properly dressed—a lightweight suit rather than casual, though.

Being less economically developed than the rest of the EEC, Greece still has a more traditional approach to business. Haggling at every level is expected (though please note, not by the police!), and even restaurants will accept a haggle over the bill. Owners do not mind your visiting their kitchens, and generally a Greek host in a restaurant he knows well will probably order the meal from there. Waiters take an active part in recommending a meal and do not just write down what you order without comment.

Food tends to turn up at the table lukewarm, even cold, and it takes a long time to consume it when you are in conversation with amiable people. Almost everything is cooked in olive oil—it's even poured over bread. Apart from not eating at all, I know of no way to avoid liberal consumption of this green oil. If you don't like olive oil, as with most unusual food in strange (to you!) places, take only small portions and eat everything, washing it down with the local wine (which in Greece can be very rough, though Demestica is passable in my view).

A lunchtime appointment can last all afternoon, assuming

that it starts anywhere near the arranged time. If Italians are sometimes slack when it comes to punctuality, Greeks appear never to have heard of the word, and they frequently end meetings quickly or let them run on for several days. (How they ever managed to become a major maritime nation with their attitude to time I don't know.)

The summer months (June through August) are dead for business in Greece (unless you are part of a Greek family), and on Wednesday afternoons you are likely to be unable to contact anybody.

Getting appointments by telephone is complicated by the fact that the telephone directory is in the Greek alphabet and will be beyond you unless you read Greek. If you need help try the receptionist at your hotel (another reason for booking into a chain hotel). I once had a receptionist in Athens spend three hours calling all the locals with the same Greek name in the phone book because I had forgotten that I could not look up the name myself (which you can do in any European country that uses our alphabet, even if you do not speak the language).

In conversation you should avoid the subject of Turkey, and if you express any views on Cyprus make sure that they take the Greek side of that bewildering and unhappy dispute. I know Turkey is a member of NATO along with Greece, but from my observation most Greeks appear to think they face greater military danger from Turkey than they do from the Soviet Union. Whatever the reason for this feeling (and I once had it explained to me for several hours in a pavement restaurant in Athens by a former Cabinet minister, but the Demestica muddled my memory and I have forgotten what he said), it is best left alone as the Greeks feel quite strongly about it and might misinterpret your comments.

Apart from shipping, air travel, and tourism, your business with Greece is likely to be in products of a less sophisticated range than you would deal in with Germany. You will find the Greeks to be reliably honest in business matters but probably less than efficient in carrying out their commitments. The Mediterranean *mañana* mood prevails in most of their dealings, but they have a traditional approach to money and know what is and what is not profitable.

This means that Greeks respect people with money, or its equivalents in the islands, such as sheep, land, olive groves, and houses. I have a Greek son-in-law, and the story of the union of the two families—including a thinly disguised appraisal of my assets by a family delegation flying over to inspect me—would fill a volume on its own. They are a very proud people, and in many respects, especially on the islands, they have values long since abandoned in the more commercialized parts of Europe.

Do not judge the wealth or success of the Greek negotiator by how he is dressed—what is comfortable for him may look rather untidy, but he could very well be a millionaire or damn close to becoming one. And don't judge a person's wealth by his or her politics. Many rich people support the leftists (it goes back to the experience of wartime fascism), though they stop short of supporting a socialist reorganization of business.

An American businessman I know who operates in the Middle East out of Athens told me that Greece is one place on the earth where the male chauvinist's adage is often true; you will seldom see a rich Greek man with an unattractive woman. His advice, as a rule of thumb, is to work backwards from the relative good looks and figure of the woman who accompanies the untidy negotiator to an estimate of his wealth or position. The trouble with this advice is that most Greek women look (at least to me) like Aphrodite no matter who they are with.

The Spanish

At the other end of the Mediterranean we find the Spanish, an altogether different people from the Greeks. Spaniards are proud, even haughty, people, much given to perceiving slights when none were intended and always behaving when they negotiate as if they own the world, or the part of it that you are in.

Unlike the Greeks, they always dress for business (and for most other occasions) and have a formal outlook on life and relationships, especially domestic arrangements, not found elsewhere in southern Europe. Hence, do not wander away from a beach or a pool dressed, or rather undressed, in swimming attire. Except in the most downbeat of tourist areas the Spaniards, and their police, are very prudish about public behavior.

To some extent it is incorrect to describe the people who live in Spain as Spaniards, and in some parts you can cause great offense by doing so. The country is regionally divided, and since Franco died its regional dissimilarities have become more pronounced, particularly among the Basques and Catalonians who live in two of the most modern and industrialized regions.

Several regions have pronounced separatist political parties represented in either local assemblies or the Madrid parliament, and it is therefore wise not to stray into Spanish local politics if you intend to do business with them. Nor is it wise to express opinions about bullfighting! The Spaniards are also very proud of their soccer teams.

They lay great stress on personal honor, and you will find that contracts entered into by them are strictly fulfilled. They expect no less from you. They have the Mediterranean knack for haggling and will do so without blushing, expecting you to do the same. But once agreed on, the contract is not to be tampered with lightly. They would rather take a loss than admit openly that they have made a mistake. Help them out (quietly) if you realize that they are suffering unintentionally from a deal, and you will win friends and allies for life.

A lot of business in Spain is either conducted or celebrated over the evening meal, and you should be aware that the Spaniards seldom sit down to eat their dinner before 9 P.M. Often it is closer to midnight and is likely to be preceded by a visit to a *tapas* bar, where you can eat some seafood snacks and drink a few glasses of beer or sherry. If your arrangements do not include a visit to a tapas, eat something earlier if you are likely to be hungry. If this is not possible, try if you can to avoid alcohol until you eat; otherwise you might well be careless when it counts.

No business is conducted in the afternoon during siesta (2 P.M. to 4 P.M.) and banks are closed after 1:30 P.M. in the summer. You too will feel better with an afternoon nap, followed by a shower to wake you up.

The Portuguese

The Portuguese, on the other hand, are a little more like the Greeks: informal, late for appointments, sociable, and, except for the very rich, as poor on the whole.

They dress much more formally than the Greeks, though, and can often be seen wearing vests on a very hot day. If your negotiating partner keeps his jacket on, you should keep yours on too. Ties are almost certain to be required on all occasions, both business and social.

All business in Portugal takes time. It is the original land of the *mañana* school of decision making. Yet there is hardly a more pleasant place to hang around doing business—the golf courses are superb, the beaches magnificent, and the dining arrangements just fine.

You should note that a lot of British business families are

active in the port trade, some having been there for generations, so if fortified wines are your business you may well be
surprised at the perfect English spoken by the "Portuguese"
negotiator.

The Dutch

The Dutch were at one time probably the most formal people in Europe, and they are certainly still the tidiest (with the
Swiss a wee skip behind). I don't know if Greece and the
Netherlands do much business, but if they do it is a triumph
of commercial spirit over cultural preference.

The Dutch older generation are ultraclean and orderly,
and they like everything in business to be likewise. They prefer to plan their business deals and the meetings that lead to
them some time in advance and are unlikely to respond positively to your calling on them without notice. You cannot
make appointments from your hotel if you have made none
before you left the United States.

They are very open and straightforward. You will see this
in the uncurtained windows of their houses. A whole family
will go about their business oblivious of the entire world
looking in on them. (Do not confuse this habit with the lit
windows with ladies in them in the red-light districts where
prostitution is legal.)

This sense of order in the over-forty generation probably
explains some part of the deliberately untidy and almost un-
washed revolt of the young against authority in the Netherlands. They have simply turned their elders' behavior upside
down in an expression of (affluent) disapproval. Their politics
appear to be anti-American, and your best response to this, if
you attract their attention, is to be ready to listen to what
they have to say and to put your own view without anger.
They appear to respect an honest difference of opinion and

will leave you alone once they see you are not overreacting to their rebellion.

Because nobody else speaks their language the Dutch speak the languages of other lands. Almost everybody you meet will speak English and/or German, so you should have no trouble negotiating with more or less total understanding of your position on the part of your Dutch partners. If they want to confer among themselves they have the advantage of being able to do so by switching to Dutch, secure in the knowledge that their adjournment discussion is private. The recent postcolonial immigration from Indonesia and Surinam has given Dutch society a more multiracial mix.

Traditionally, the Dutch have been very good with money and very conscious of its proper management, until perhaps recently when they have begun to spread around their tax income from North Sea gas with a very "un-Dutch" casual abandon. You should remember that the politics of this bonanza distribution are strictly the business of the Dutch people, who are not altogether anxious to receive your generous advice or criticism (though the Dutch willingly talk about politics and the bewildering array of parties in their government).

The Dutch are very good business negotiators, though they are a trifle ruthless when given their head. They think they can handle foreigners quite well and tend not to be nationalistic about the Netherlands (though they do not like to hear their country called "Holland," which in fact refers to a couple of the provinces and not to the entire country). As citizens of a small and vulnerable country they are the most European of all the members of the EEC and can be impatient with overly nationalistic people from elsewhere in Europe.

Several of Europe's largest corporations have strong Dutch connections (Philips, Shell, and Unilever, for example). The Dutch are very good at building international business links.

They are very competitive—look at their ship salvage businesses, for instance—and they have a Germanic passion for
getting the contract right. They will exercise any economic
leverage they can on you to secure additional advantages.
Dutch salvage captains are sometimes criticized (probably
unjustly) for waiting near a ship in difficulty until its owners
agree to their terms.

The Belgians

Across the border, the Belgians combine some of the characteristics of the Dutch with some of the French. To the north
of Brussels the country is populated by the Flemish, a Dutch
offshoot from previous centuries, and to the south of the capital there are the French-speaking Belgians. Both communities have been locked into a highly complicated rivalry for
many years, the details of which are not really your business
and are best steered clear of.

The Belgian firm will more than likely have different people responsible for each sector of the country or will confine
itself to one part or the other, in which case you will need to
find another company in the other part. Finding an address
while driving can be hazardous as there are very few road
signs in the cities (for street names look for tiny plates on the
sides of buildings), and those that are available are often
painted over by people militantly supporting the other language.

Belgians have a French proclivity for shaking hands whenever and wherever they meet or say good-bye. They will do
so with colleagues even when leaving the office. You can
never shake hands too often in Belgium (or France).

Brussels is not just the capital of Belgium. It is also the lo-
cation of the main administrative offices of the European
Economic Community and the headquarters of the North

Atlantic Treaty Organization (NATO). This means that a high proportion of the city's accommodation is taken up with resident and visiting bureaucrats, delegations, lobbyists, and demonstrators. Of the latter the farmers are the most agitated and it is best to avoid Brussels when the press announce that European (especially French) farmers are marching on the EEC buildings. Peace rallies can also be disruptive, though these are less frequent.

The Belgians love to mix business with pleasure. They entertain a lot and like to be entertained. This is one country where your expense account is going to be raided up to its limit. The influx of international civil and military bureaucrats and the politicians that go with them, all spending their generous expense allowances, has made food very expensive. If invited out by your negotiating partners do not hit the menu as if you have not eaten for a week, and if you invite them out you can pray that they will do the same for you!

Two small social points for drinkers. First, "beer" in English sounds to a Belgian waiter like "Byrrh," an altogether different drink—ask for, say, "Stella Artois" (or just "Stella"), which is a strongish version of American beer. Second, "Scotch" is a well-known brand name for a local beer, not a whiskey. If you want Scotch "whisky" ask for a "whisky" or ask for one by its brand name (Johnnie Walker or whatever).

I once was negotiating in Bruges with a Belgian law firm about an indemnity my client had rashly signed, when my opposite number suggested we go to a "little night club" he knew. I agreed, being tired and thirsty. He didn't mention that the club was in a large mansion near Maastricht in the Netherlands, à long drive away, and, once there, he clearly intended staying until breakfast time the next day. My feeble protests were overruled, and we got back to my hotel in time for lunch, followed by a further round of negotiations that afternoon.

So make sure you are fit and hearty before negotiating with Belgians, or better still avoid the social life until after the deal is settled.

As in the Netherlands, if you are in a street with ladies sitting perfectly still in lit windows you are in the red light district. Prostitution in these places is legal and supervised, but like anywhere else in the world you are at risk in a health, if not a moral, sense.

The Scandinavians

As you go north in Europe you meet entirely different cultures. Collectively, the Norwegians, Danes, and Swedes are known as Scandinavians, and on the surface they have a great deal in common with each other and with the Finns. When you get to know them you will begin to discern subtle differences, including the fact that they live in separate countries and have their own parliaments. Their countries, however, form a Nordic Council which makes them all free trade areas for each other's goods.

On the whole Scandinavians are very civil, very polite, and mostly formal in their relationships with foreigners. When they are together they tend to loosen up a bit, which is why their governments, if only to dampen their citizens' exuberance, have adopted extremely harsh drinking laws. Never drink *anything* alcoholic and drive a car in Scandinavia; the police and local courts are *never* sympathetic, and it will cost you enormous inconvenience to say the least. The fact that you are a foreigner will not protect you from a mandatory jail sentence.

Booze is extremely expensive in Scandinavia. The price of a glass of French brandy would buy you a bottle in France. Hence, when you visit any Scandinavian country take in with you a full customs allowance of Scotch (malt whiskey preferably). This makes an excellent gift to your negotiating partner (after the deal if it's the first time—before if it's a regular visit). The local price of a bottle of Scotch is prohibitive (and is meant to be), and your partner will be more than grateful. If he or she offers to pay for it, decline firmly and put it down to your PR budget.

Business lunches are largely a sandwich affair—the selection of meats, salmon, and cheeses is extensive. Dinners are much more traditional, however, and you should note that the main course is often repeated after everybody has cleared their first helping. Hence, go easy on the roast potatoes and leave room for a second serving of venison or beef steaks. Entertaining is expensive—more so than in other parts of Europe partly, but not entirely, because of the price of drinks.

A great deal of alcohol can be consumed at a business dinner, but either everybody will order a taxi to go home in or each car pool will have its nondrinking driver "volunteered" for the evening. There is no way that you will persuade a Scandinavian to have "one for the road," and it is regarded as extremely ill-mannered to attempt to do so. They have to live with their country's drinking laws after you have gone home and whatever they remark about these laws privately, they rigorously obey them.

Sweden has an affluent population. Its wage costs are comparatively high, and it can only survive economically by a deliberate policy of specialization. They are very serious about their business and invest heavily in modern technology to make sure that they are competitive around the world.

They will buy from you if you supply top-quality, excellent products that they need and that they cannot get locally; top quality is certainly what they will sell to you. The Swedes exist in world trade through the sheer excellence of their products, and they seek high-value specialized segments of the markets that they export to rather than mass-volume low-margin sales in markets that their larger rivals triumph in.

Scandinavians do not go in for long price haggles, and they

expect that your proposition will be thoroughly worked out before it is presented to them. What changes they require will probably be minor. On the whole if they are doing business with you at all it is because they have identified you as an expert firm in your market, and they will expect your proposition to be the best that is available. If they see glaring holes in your proposition they will revise their estimate of your professionalism and probably take their business elsewhere rather than argue with you over details which they think you ought to have got right the first time.

Swedes and Norwegians have a special problem in motivating their people to try harder to achieve more than they are already doing. I think this has something to do with the tax laws. Their governments have gone in for the redistribution of income in a big way (from the highest and purest of motives). This tends to produce executives who reach for a level of achievement and then settle down to that level without pushing for more, because the rewards for higher effort are perceived to be worth a lot less than the extra effort. Tax evasion has not been a problem in the past, but my contacts in Norway have remarked that there is a growing "black" economy associated with the oil boom and the influx of foreign employees.

The entrepreneurial energies of Scandinavians have tended recently to be confined to protecting what they have rather than directed to expanding into where they could be; it is more common to find a Swedish or Norwegian firm fighting hard to cut costs in established product lines than it is to find them fighting for new business.

I was advising a Swedish company in 1982 that was preparing for a major renegotiation of an important contract, and I was surprised to find that the entire discussion of the top executives was concentrated on what concessions they would have to make to keep the contract (clearly they wanted the business at any price). Nothing was being done to develop an alternative in case they didn't keep it even on their surrender terms. If they had spent some time on the latter they might have discovered some backbone to keep the contract on favorable, that is, profitable, terms.

They are not averse, however, to investing heavily in new technology (computers and satellites) if it helps them to stay ahead in their established markets, such as shipping. Several U.S. firms have established themselves in these areas.

On the import side they seek high-quality luxury consumer goods to meet the demands of their affluent citizens, but be warned. The high costs of distribution (especially wage and tax costs) compel them to squeeze hard on your price if they are to achieve the necessary markup on sales to ensure that they can cover their costs and make a small profit.

In Finland, where four large chains dominate the retail trade, you will have to compete very hard on price and quality to get your products into the shops, given the extensive competition and a preference in the stores for buying local.

The affluence of the Scandinavian countries gives you your opportunity. On the one hand their citizens have a lot to spend, and on the other they are forced, through high domestic labor costs, to import high-volume high-quality products that they find uneconomical to produce themselves.

The sauna to Scandinavians is what the siesta is to Spaniards, Greeks, and Venezuelans. It's an integral part of their lives. You should be sure to experience a sauna during your visits if only to be able to say in conversation that you had one during your stay. Most good hotels have saunas, and you can experiment there in a safe environment.

In the sauna—a northern version of the Turkish bath—you will experience great heat, but you can leave any time you feel uncomfortable and cool down. If you can try the sauna on your own during the first days of a visit (or even at your local sauna in the United States, though you should note that

HOW NOT TO TACKLE A SUSPECTED RIPOFF

I was minding my own business at Gothenburg airport when I was approached by a businessman who asked if I was traveling first class and if I was would I join him for a drink (I said yes to both questions). He wanted to talk about something that was exciting him greatly, and when he heard I was a consultant negotiator his tale poured forth.

Briefly, his story was that he had been selling children's clothes to a Swedish chain store for three years. On this visit he had arrived early and had taken time out to casually wander through one of the branches of this chain. Naturally, he had gravitated to the children's department and looked for his company's products.

What do you think he found? Right! His clothes were there and were prominently displayed. This pleased him immensely, and in his pride he informed the staff that he owned the firm that made what they were selling. They were most impressed and told him that there was a steady demand for his clothes, given their excellent quality.

He was in turn even more pleased at this news, and after a while he left. One thing, however, stuck in his mind, and that was the price tag on one of his lines. It wasn't until he left that he realized that the Swedish krona price represented in dollars a markup of several hundred percent on his selling price to the store.

Such was his concern that he went back to the shop and noted down the prices of every one of his products. He worked out the markup and found it was consistent throughout. The chain store, which had always pleaded poverty and tight competition as reasons for squeezing his prices, was, he said, "Ripping me off."

He was upset about this, even though the price he had gotten for his products was profitable to his business. He raised this immediately with the Swedish firm later that morning, and told them he felt they had been cheating him. They were obviously offended at this charge, but after much discussion they agreed to raise their purchase prices. They claimed this would squeeze their profits because of their very high labor costs and the taxes on their stores.

He was now even more worried, because he felt he had overreacted and gone in too strong and perhaps had damaged his good relationship. I suggested it would have been better if he had raised the question of the store's retail pricing policy quite neutrally and let the implications of that lead them to either a credible defense of their markup or to a revision of their purchase price. By charging in he had risked causing offense when none was necessary, and whatever he had gained on the present trip might be followed by a falling off in orders as they eased out an obviously disgruntled supplier. By paying him more they had partly confirmed his feeling of being cheated, whether this was the case or not.

in Scandinavia saunas are *not* surrogate sex parlors!) you will be better able to accept an invitation to a sauna from a business partner, which is a sure sign that you are being well received. In Finland, a post-deal sauna is almost mandatory, so be ready for the second most enjoyable experience in your life.

You will not be expected to compete with your partner in the temperature that you can take or the time that you can take it. There is no loss of face if you must retire to the cooling pool before he does. After all, he has been acclimatized to the sauna over many years. It is unlikely that you will have enough energy—let alone oxygen!—to negotiate in a sauna, so don't bother trying.

The British

Turning to Britain and its negotiating styles we can discern certain basic characteristics common to all of its component parts. You should always remember that the United Kingdom consists of four nations, not just one, and that they are molded more or less firmly together.

The dominant nation is, of course, England. In fact much of the rest of the world refers to England when they really mean the United Kingdom (L'Angleterre and so on). To be fair, most English people automatically speak of England when meaning Britain, and in doing so when it is not appropriate they are unintentionally insensitive about the feelings of the Scots, Welsh, and Irish. So don't refer to a Scot as English!

The British share a common trait, which is that they have a wholly justified reputation for one business practice above all others. They have a near-perfect record for the late delivery of almost every product they produce. This is the single most consistent complaint of foreign importers of British goods, and it is heard right across the surface of the planet.

Much has been written about this problem in the United Kingdom, and much effort has been put into doing something about it. But it stubbornly refuses to be improved upon quickly and anyway, the idea is so entrenched in modern export folklore that even if the situation was improved upon it would still take years, if not generations, to eradicate it from the minds of customers all over the world.

Why does Britain have this deserved reputation? I do not know. Many U.S. and Japanese subsidiaries have managed to get their delivery dates from their British plants up to international standards, but even Ford and General Motors have failed to eradicate the problem completely.

This always poses a problem when British managers are negotiating abroad. Having an identified weakness means that a negotiator is on the defensive and often has to accept terms for business that would otherwise be onerous. Negotiators can impose a delivery penalty on a British contract because it is credible for them to insist upon one. A British promise to deliver on time invites the response, "If you do deliver on time then you don't need to fear the penalty, but if you fear the penalty you are obviously unsure of your delivery."

When British companies had a worldwide lead in technology (Britain was the first economy to industrialize in the early nineteenth century) and a relative monopoly position in the old colonial Empire, they probably got into a habit of caring less about delivery than they ought to have. After Hitler's war, from 1945 to about 1955, Britain once again had a substantial captive market, with many of its rivals out of business until they repaired war damage. Again, the fact of being able to sell everything they could produce did little to wake the British up to the essential requirements of a modern trading nation.

If delivery was the only criterion for trade, the United Kingdom would suffer a catastrophic collapse in its exports until it did something about its failings. Fortunately, delivery is only one of several aspects of British production, and in many cases it is not the all-important one.

Britain is a major trading nation; though its share of the growing volume of world trade is falling, it is still expanding its absolute output of exports. Two reasons among others for this credible performance are the technical competence in its industries and the sheer inventiveness of its scientific and engineering people. These strengthen the hands of negotiators plying their products across the world.

Technology is no longer monopolized by the British, however, and there is a warning here in the so-called "sunrise" industries (communications, for example); Britain may not have the technical capacity to keep its share of world trade from declining very rapidly once new technologies pass to rivals.

Until that unhappy (for the British) outcome, negotiations are by no means a one-way street for them. Being clobbered with "low delivery morale" (in other words, Britain's trading partners do not believe what they are promised) and countering with technological excellence is a regular experience for British negotiators dealing with the rest of the world. As long as they can keep the balance between their company's strengths and weaknesses in their favor they will be around the international trading scene for long enough.

It is only recently, incidentally, that the majority of export-oriented business negotiators have developed a consistent policy of face-to-face contact with their clients in foreign climes. There is no doubt that U.S. companies have been poor at regular service visits compared to their rivals. Partly, it is in response to the very good records of their rivals in this respect that U.S. firms have begun to change. And there is no doubt that if you want to maintain high sales volume in export markets, regular high-level visits are essential. Not only does it do you good with a client, it also does you good indirectly by bolstering the status and morale of your local agents.

This leads to another weakness of the U.S. negotiator, namely the lack of a proclivity for languages other than English. There is a minor arrogance about speakers of English as a mother tongue; they assume that everybody else in the world knows, or wants to know, how to speak English. They are not going to change quickly (nor are they encouraged to do so by the behavior of the rest of the world, which learns English as a second language—with the exception, of course, of the French, who especially insist on speaking French with English-speaking visitors).

Negotiations with British firms, naturally, will take place in English, literature will be printed in English, and with many firms little compromise will be visible in the matter of things foreign.

Of the people who make up Britain, the English, being the largest in population (46 millon out of 54 million), are the ones who set the pace in international business. The English have a reputation for being gentlemen (generally very honest in their dealings even when things go against them), though for the most part they are merely amateurs. More than 80 percent of British managers, for instance, are totally unqualified—only 7 percent have university degrees. Their approach to business is well short of professional standards, and they compare badly with overseas executives.

This means that they appear at negotiations poorly prepared, can be inflexible in the critical phases (repackaging and bargaining), and do not exert much energy. It is no accident that most of the high-profile successful entrepreneurs in the United Kingdom are not native born (Robert Maxwell, Tiny Roland, Charles Forte, Rupert Murdoch, and Nazmu Virani, to name a few). The lack of, or rather decline in, managerial flair is nowhere better demonstrated than in the successful emergence of post-war immigrant shopkeepers and small businessmen as displacers of indigenous owners. It is worth noting the number of British citizens happily, and successfully, working in the United States, which suggests that the problem is cultural rather than something inbred.

Amateurism in business management is seen in the stubbornness of British negotiators—an almost take-it-or-leave-it attitude. No wonder so many traditional businesses have succumbed to takeovers and reorganization by entrepreneurs who have understood the changing markets of the world and are ready to try something new. Poor investment, indifferent quality, poor delivery, and unreliability are not features that give grounds for pride.

If a British firm could get these factors right, it might do wonders in the world. The fact that so many deals concluded by British negotiators do make a profit and do win repeat business suggests that the British are not entirely hopeless. It is, however, a national characteristic to be self-effacing when not self-denigrating.

As for the Scots, they divide into two groups: those that live and work in Scotland and those that live and work in other parts of the world. Of the first group, we can assume that they are fairly well resourced in a financial sense. This tends to make them very cautious, sometimes beyond the point where enterprise can flourish. The second group often rise high in their adopted communities while keeping their financial sense about them.

There are relatively few opportunities to run a really large business in Scotland. Its economic base is one-tenth of that of the United Kingdom, and much of its key industry is run from elsewhere in the world; only the financial center of Edinburgh is an exception to this rule, and many of its funds are sent elsewhere. Thus many of the most talented negotiators emigrate, and they exercise their hard-headed talent for business in their new environment. This can lead to very successful business careers.

Scots will always concentrate on the financial apects of a deal ("We're in it for the money, not the glory!"), but having little to trade they are in the smaller leagues internationally.

It is not really necessary to translate American names for things into English. An American who refers to the elevator, the sidewalk, the automobile, and the gas station is unlikely to be misunderstood anywhere in Britain. In fact, translating words deliberately would risk appearing to be patronizing. British television has spread the American version of English into the humblest of homes, and there is no risk of confusing anybody, especially during a business negotiation.

Speaking the same language—well, almost the same language—especially during a business trip including the European mainland, where you have required translation services, is likely to make you more talkative in the company of British negotiators. But beware of straying into certain areas of conversation, such as Ireland's future, the benefits of a republic over a monarchy, George III, the way you would run Britain's economy, who does most in NATO, and why the British Empire ended.

Safer topics include the weather, Britain's heritage, and the Royal Family (note that there is no such title as "the Queen of England," especially in Wales or Scotland; she is known as "the Queen" or, to be formal, "the Queen of the United Kingdom of Great Britain and Northern Ireland"). If your forebears were from Britain it is always acceptable to say so, particularly if they were Scottish, no matter how tenuous the connection—even your spouse's forebears can be claimed as your own.

Not much business is undertaken during the summer months—from when the schools close in early July to the end of August—or, increasingly, over the Christmas to New Year period. Business resumes in England by January 2 but rarely in Scotland before January 4. On business trips you will find it is possible to play a round or so of golf on famous courses for a token payment, and a lot of business is contracted between the first and the eighteenth (sometimes the "nineteenth") holes.

In general, except in the very best of establishments, you should not expect the same standards of personal service as are common in hotels, restaurants, and stores in the United States. On the other hand, you should not make a noisy fuss about this as it is not a personal slight against you.

One reason why the British are so addicted to forming (sullen) lines is that they have lower expectations of being attended to than most other nations. As you can't beat the system, join it, especially if a line has formed, as hell hath no fury like a British line when a foreigner queue jumps!

The European tribes

Doing business with the European tribes ought to be equivalent to doing business in the multitrillion-dollar economy of

TIPS FOR TRAVELERS IN EUROPE

The four best entry points into Europe are Schiphol, Amsterdam; Heathrow, London; Frankfurt, Germany; and Charles de Gaulle, Paris. All have excellent connections to almost anywhere else. Schiphol is probably the best to wait around in, followed by Frankfurt. If a long wait is required at Heathrow, get a courtesy coach outside the terminal building to a local airport hotel and wait there.

Driving can be a problem. In Britain they drive on the "wrong" side of the road and this takes some getting used to. In Italy, the roads are a racetrack—drivers don't worry about what is happening behind them, or what their own vehicles force other vehicles to do to avoid them. All attention is on what is happening in front of them. They drive very fast, have no lane discipline, and do not wait for lights to change before moving. In France they drive very fast on the main highways, and trucks will pass you doing 80 miles per hour plus. In Germany there is no speed limit on the autobahns, and you will be bumped from behind if you do not let a vehicle pass you. Accidents can get you jailed until everything is sorted out in Spain, Yugoslavia, and Scandinavia, particularly if there is any indication of alcohol. If you hire an automobile and cross over between Britain (including Ireland) and the continent, remember that your driving lights will be pointing the "wrong way" and that this will annoy oncoming drivers. Get advice from the car rental people about this problem.

Many countries require you to leave your passport with your hotel's reception while they register you with the local police. In Britain they will require you to supply your passport number when you register at the hotel.

Police behavior varies, but the safest rule is *never* to argue with a police officer, even if you are innocent. If it's serious you will be allowed (eventually) to contact the nearest U.S. embassy. In Britain, the police are unarmed, but they are armed elsewhere.

the United States, except that the barriers to business within Europe, including within the EEC countries, mean that there is nothing like the freedom of doing business between the states of the U.S. of A. The customs union of the EEC now has bigger and more intrusive customs procedures than those that existed when the countries were entirely separate! Harmonization of business practice across separate units is a long way from being achieved in the EEC countries as it has been in the United States.

This leads business negotiators not just to need the skills of trading and bargaining but also requires of them that they immerse themselves in the cultural and business norms of each country.

Given that learning a country's language is conducive to learning how to negotiate with the people who speak it, those continental negotiators who have a facility for learning their neighbors' languages are much better placed to do business in Europe than Americans who tend to be ignorant of any language but their own. How long this will continue in light of the increasing intra-European trade remains to be seen, but for the moment the other Europeans have an advantage.

That the old barriers between the tribes of Europe might break down is still only a possibility for the more distant future, but two things are certain. First, if harmonization does occur it will still be shaded by the individualism of the originating countries (you will still know the difference between doing business in Greece and Norway, for example); and, second, it won't happen in a hurry.

ANSWERS TO SELF-ASSESSMENT TEST 8

1 **a** Very good! German companies often try this one, knowing that they are good payers and that foreigners like to do business with them. (Many companies believe that a German clientele is a good advertisement for them.) If you can't say no, try *c*.   (**10**)

b You are the kind of negotiator that the Germans like to do business with—it makes up for those others who know what their products are worth. If the Germans could get your steel at home they would not bother dealing with you.   **(−10)**
c At least you are trying to limit the damage. It is always best to make a conditional proposition, even if you are surrendering!   **(5)**

2 a A risky policy, as it may cause a breakdown in your long-term relationship. They may have a good reason for a pricing policy that involves an 800 percent markup. If they raise their purchase price this will confirm to you that they are ripping you off; if they don't you will still be unhappy.   **(−10)**
b A safe policy, though it leaves you without information regarding your case for a price increase.   **(5)**
c Probably the most sensible first move, to be followed by *b*. Since you have raised this issue without prompting they may wonder why you have done so, and if they are cheating you their embarrassment might show. At the next price negotiation they have the face-saving option of raising your prices.   **(10)**
d The rational move, but in business nobody likes to get less than they can. If you follow this policy either you are ripping *them* off or you have saintly tendencies!   **(7)**

3 a Only if the pound is riding high.   **(−5)**
b Not really a problem. The British government has a habit of throwing money at potential customers—it has been known to borrow money from the Swiss at 14 percent and lend it to the Poles at 7 percent to pay British shipbuilders to supply the Poles with already heavily subsidized ships. If the Communists can get deals like that, how do you rate your chances?   **(−15)**
c Absolutely right. The worst problem of British exports is simply delivery on time and when agreed. If you don't impose penalty payments on the British for poor delivery—which will almost certainly have to be paid to you and which will therefore reduce the actual cost of the products—you are simply not trying.   **(10)**
d Not really. British products are generally of high quality and advanced technology. This is often sufficient compensation for poor delivery.   **(−10)**

CHAPTER 9

Land of the Greased Palm—or, How It Is When You Trade in the Third World

The bad news

First, we should dispose of the bad news. The Third World (broadly, such countries as Ghana, Nigeria, Mali, Uganda, Zimbabwe, Kenya, Liberia, Egypt, Jordan, Malaysia, Indonesia, India, Pakistan, Thailand, the Philippines, Jamaica, Peru, and Ecuador) is a long way from being a happy and prosperous place in which to do business. Apart from having some of the worst poverty on the planet (although all, or even the majority, of the nations are not by any means starving), some of the worst records on health and hygiene, many of the worst records on education and welfare, and a long history of neglect and failure, the countries that the Third World comprises also have an unenviable record for both local violence and general warfare.

Since 1945 the majority of wars (119 out of 124 by one calculation) have taken place in the Third World; most of its systems of government are of military origin; and many of the governments that have come to power there have done so not by means of an election but through military coups or violent civil wars and revolution.

[test appears on following page]

SELF-ASSESSMENT TEST 9

1 You are stopped by a policeman in Ogoland, and he demands that you pay him 50 quonks (about 4 dollars) not to book you for speeding. You were almost stationary at the time and could not have been speeding at all. Do you tell him:

a Not before you see your consul?
b You do not pay bribes?
c Certainly, if he has change for a 100 quonk note?

2 A Nigerian importer of household paraffin-driven electricity generators with whom you have dealt successfully in the past places an order worth 230,000 dollars and requires deliveries to commence in three months. He agrees to pay against invoices on dispatch and requires an unconditional performance bond from you for 10 percent of the value of the order. Do you:

a Agree, providing he opens a confirmed, irrevocable letter of credit through your own bank for the 230,000 dollars payable on dispatch of the first batch of generators?
b Decline to sign an unconditional performance bond that is payable on demand?
c Agree because you desperately need his business to avoid major layoffs in your plant?

3 An Indian importer owes you 100,000 dollars and you demand payment before any more shipments take place. He tells you he is going through a short-term cash flow crisis and needs more time to pay, and that he cannot pay if he does not get more of your products. Do you:

a Tell him he cannot get more deliveries unless he pays what he owes?
b Tell him that if he does not pay you will sue him?
c Decide to visit him in India and see for yourself what his financial situation is really like?
d Tell him if he pays you 20,000 dollars on account you will make another delivery?

Hence, low levels of personal income, political instability, and local violence are features of the Third World that have to be borne in mind by the international business negotiator contemplating business in these countries. Legal foundations for conducting business have been laid in most of these countries, and in many of them there is more than a semblance of law and order. But the fact remains that there are wide variations in standards and conduct, and it is not always possible to seek, let alone get, redress for breaches of contract. In fact, in some places even to seek redress is to invite judicial and extrajudicial reprisals against one's business and, sometimes, one's person.

The scale of corruption

Standards of public service in respect to personal ethics and morality are not always of the kind that is expected by a person living in a relatively uncorrupt Western democracy. It is always dangerous to generalize about moral issues (let him who is without guilt first cast a stone), and you are not advised to do so except in an abstract fashion and while safely in your own backyard. But corruption, the great unacknowledged feature of business in the Third World, is a reality of business there which few are prepared for when they are confronted with its scale and, what appears to be worse, its total acceptance as a way of life.

In corrupt societies (that is, those judged to be corrupt by normal American standards, though be careful of being too pompous about this in case tomorrow's papers expose some local seandal in the United States) the norm is for almost everybody who has some discretionary power, no matter how trivial, to use that discretion to personal advantage in return for some small, or not so small, consideration. A passport gets stamped faster if a small token payment (called "dash" in West Africa) is left within the pages when it is handed over.

Otherwise, you might be left till the end of the line even if you were first to get to the counter. Similar procedures apply in customs, immigration, and the baggage reclaim area.

Success in securing airline reservations tends to be correlated with small bribes to the booking clerks; seat reservations likewise. Anything that needs rubber-stamping is a gold mine to the clerk who has the rubber stamp. If he has to consult another clerk's list or check with a supervisor, you had better bear this in mind when handing over the bribe, because what is divided by two or three is often not enough to generate an interest in your interests in those with no incentive to take an interest in your interests!

Hotel reservations can appear at the drop of a 100 cedi note and disappear if somebody got there before you with a 200 cedi note. The elevator shaft vista awaits those foolish enough to trust to their confirmed reservation for the ocean view, if they forget to dash the desk clerk. A table by the toilets in the restaurant is your best bet if you forget to look after the head waiter, and you might as well be in the toilet if you forget to demonstrate to the waiters serving the tables your goodwill and intention to see them taken care of (the best way to ensure service is to tip them when they take the order and imply that there is more to follow).

As for official forms, you have little hope of even getting near one in many countries without paying the local "tax" on the forms which are a devolved responsibility of the clerk who collects them. Pay up and you get the form; don't and you will wait, perhaps forever.

Risks of mishandling the payoff

Once petty corruption becomes a way of life and spreads right across the entire fabric of a society, it is something you have to accept as a visitor if you wish to do any business at all. You should take local guidance on the state of affairs regarding corruption and follow the advice of the old hands.

It is not only an expensive business but also a risky one. If you assume everybody is corrupt and they are not, you might get into serious trouble for attempting to bribe an honest clerk or, worse for you, an honest policeman. Several businessmen at any one time are in local jails for trying to corrupt officialdom. Perhaps the (corrupt) authorities are trying to make an example of them for PR purposes, or perhaps the businessmen did not offer a big enough bribe in the negotiations and they are in jail for the "insult."

A stranger in a Third World country has no means of knowing whether the police (or army) have stopped him or her for a real offense or because they want to collect some extra pocket money.

Two basic rules should be applied in these circumstances. First, and without exception, you should never stand on your dignity and imply either by word, grimace, or gesture that the official who has stopped you does not have authority to do so, or that he is in any way unsuited to be in the position he is in, or that he is in some sense incompetent, a candidate for the gestapo, or typical of his race, religion, or nation. Second, you must not make a direct approach to the subject of bribery unless, as can happen, they tell you straight out ("Dash me, man!") that they want some payoff for letting you go. In this case, pay up and go.

Your best bet, when not sure of the scene, is to apologize for whatever wrong they claim that you have committed (even if you feel indignant because of your saintlike innocence) and say words to this effect: "I am a stranger in your country, officer, sir, and I am very sorry for my mistake, sir. In my country we pay on-the-spot fines for similar offenses, and if you tell me, sir, what the fine is, I will pay it to you immediately, sir."

Either (unlikely) he will tell you that you do not pay fines on the spot in Ogoland but will have to appear in court next

Monday and pay any fine then, or (more likely) he will tell you what you have to pay him. As long as you go through the above with no money in sight (don't reach into your pocket for your wallet until told to do so), you are unlikely to be charged with attempting to bribe an officer of the law. If he asks you for money and you pay him you are unlikely to have further trouble.

So keep your smart comments to yourself, dash them, and get going.

If you cannot bring yourself to do this, well and good. But in that case be ready for a long hassle, an uncomfortable time in detention, and perhaps, in some countries, a few indignities and bruises to your person. While these are going on you may wish to review your decision to be an international negotiator in the Third World.

Rackets in quotas, permissions, and licenses

In India, up until recently, public corruption was so widespread that it was a safe bet that you could offer a bribe—even for a train ticket—and expect to get appropriate treatment. Many members of India's many governments are widely suspected of being involved in big payoffs from this or that interest to smooth the way over the many obstacles to the conduct of business that have been created by India's central government.

Believing, as it does, that intervention is necessary if India is to be developed industrially and commercially, the government in New Delhi has introduced thousands of regulations and licenses for all forms of trade, including exports and imports. These have become bonanzas for the officials who have discretion on how the regulations are applied and to whom the licenses are doled out.

Whenever a government is persuaded by somebody to

have a quota for this or that (in the "national interest") it creates a meal ticket for the clerk who has control of the quotas. In Nigeria and Ghana businesses have grown up in the trading of licenses and quotas, not of the goods that are meant to be licensed or quota-ed! An official quota to import shoes is traded across the business community for fabulous sums long before a single pair of shoes reaches the country. I know one businessman in Ghana who bought the production license for shirts and is sitting on it until somebody else comes along to buy it at a price considerably more profitable to him than actually laying out the capital to make shirts would be.

When somebody does come along who wants to manufacture shirts he will still have to get permission to erect the buildings. That permission too could provide a good living for the person who gets hold of it first, without them ever having to go through the trauma of actually building and operating a manufacturing plant.

Negotiating in these conditions to set up an import distribution network for your shoes, or a plant to manufacture them locally, is not going to be a simple process of putting a proposition to somebody and letting him evaluate the commercial prospects. You will have no idea how serious the opposite number is about actually doing anything about your proposition. He may only be interested in tying you into a commitment to secure the appropriate paper license for somebody (anybody!) to implement your proposition so that he can resell the license to a third party.

If the project is complex and on a large scale, the number of officials that have to be squared can reach formidable levels. The costs of seeing them all taken care of will not be trivial and for that reason, they are not likely to be accountable. That is, you have no assurance of the efficiency of your bribes or whether the people whom you thought, or were persuaded to believe, needed to be squared received anything at all. You could be the victim of a con as well as a can-

HEALTH, TRAVEL, AND HAPPINESS

I know several U.S. expatriates who made lucrative livings from acting as middlemen between "associates" of the Kenyan government and major overseas investors in Kenya. Some of them found they could not get their wealth out of Kenya when they came to retire. They thus face the rest of their lives in lonely but affluent splendor in Nairobi or Mombasa (with the real attendant risk of being exposed and expelled as the old elite moves over), when in fact they would rather return relatively rich and more or less safe to where they hail from.

In the interest of international understanding, I agreed to help one of these gentlemen develop a scheme to get as much of his money out of Kenya as was possible, without his risking losing the lot if he was caught trying to do so. I also insisted that my scheme would not be illegal.

My plan involved the use of the so-called "medical expenses" dodge and a sideline deal in unused airline tickets. My fee for this service was to be 5 percent of the gross amount he got out of Kenya plus expenses.

First, he needed a local Kenyan doctor to certify him as a heart patient who needed urgent medical attention in the United States, easily achieved on the old hands' circuit.

Then I had to find someone in America who would agree to "treat" him for his complaint. The catch was that he was to "need" treatment regularly—every three months, in Boston—and the doctor was to charge a large fee each time. On each trip he was also allowed to take some personal income for expenses.

The difference between the fee actually paid to the doctor and the invoice charged on my client's bank in Nairobi was to be paid into my client's bank account in the United States.

The second part of the plan involved my client's purchasing in Kenya first-class round-the-world tickets each time he and his wife had to fly to Boston for his "medical" attention. He would use these tickets to get to Boston and I would place the unused portion of the ticket with a pal in the travel business at a discount price.

The unused portion was sold to a manager of an international export business who used the discounted (first-class) tickets to fly to various parts of the world. Airlines will not refund cash for air tickets sold in Third World countries but did, at that time, allow various changes of destination and dates of travel on the tickets as long as the overall price was not altered (although recently even this dodge was stopped if the tickets were issued in certain countries); and they seldom take any notice of the name on the ticket.

After a year of using this plan my pal managed to extract over 152,000 dollars net into the United States. Naturally I wanted my 5 percent of the gross amount plus my expenses.

So if any reader knows the whereabouts of a certain "gentleman" recently resident in Kenya who is in excellent health and has a pocketful of first-class round-the-world tickets for sale, I would appreciate it greatly if you would pass his present address on to me. He owes me about 10,000 dollars!

Moral: If you arrange cash deals, get paid cash, preferably in advance (on the hookers' principle), and always as you go along, especially when dealing with "pals."

---

didate to become a convict (and in much of Africa there are more con men out of jail than in it).

The market in official permissions is only one side of the deal. In many areas where central control is not as strong and certain as it should be (and sometimes even under the very noses of official personnel) you might be subject to an unofficial market in permissions.

You will have to pay off the local bosses (or those who convince you that they are local bosses) or suffer the risk of severe retribution to your person and property. (If your trucks are burned out you'll know they were not kidding you.) Lawlessness of this kind is a natural by-product of the system of official corruption. For the unofficial "tax" collectors who do not have an official gold mine of discretion at their disposal, the remedy is to invent one and where necessary to back it up with threats, intimidation, and outright violence.

If all this seems incredible, you should consider the well-known operations of the Mafia in parts of southern Italy and the payoffs they require in addition to whatever permissions you have obtained from the authorities. You might also consider the very large-scale operations of the "godfathers" of Northern Ireland who "tax" all kinds of businesses, allegedly to replenish their paramilitary funds but more often to support their personal life-styles—and this with the armed authorities patrolling the streets looking for them!

Large-scale projects are likely to be negotiated at the highest levels. Nobody ever did much in the way of large-scale projects in Kenya who did not pass before the presidential desk when Jomo Kenyatta (and Mrs. Kenyatta!) ran the show. President Sadat's Egypt was similar, though the front man there was his brother, while in the Philippines everything has been run for many years through President and Mrs. Marcos.

In Nicaragua the Somoza family ran the entire country as if it was a private bank account. They went to such excesses that most of the population preferred to take their chances with the Communists rather than continue to live under the family's rule. This shows how desperate they must have been, for Communists in power are every bit as despotic as those they throw out, only worse, for no Communist government has ever demitted office once it has established itself.

If you are dealing with the top you can be sure of at least one thing. If you get the go-ahead the project is likely to become a reality eventually, though if they tap your brain and discover that they can do the job themselves and skim off the profits, you might find yourself the creator of a good idea and persona non grata on an early flight home.

You may need presidential-level approval to get an otherwise lethargic system to move in your favor. But presidents and their families cannot supervise everything, and you will have to rely on people a little lower in the structure to get things really moving. This might cost you. (I avoid any reference at all to what presidential approval could cost you in some countries and in the interests of not having a future visa blocked, certainly cast no aspersions on the countries mentioned above!)

First World corruption too

Before you start feeling a little smug about all this frank talk of corruption in Third World countries, you should pause a little and look around the First World. There are scams everywhere. The only difference is that most of them are unusual, and in the United States those who indulge in them are chased and prosecuted if caught.

By way of illustration, I read of a restaurant in Hollywood where the rich, famous, and glamorous (and those who wanted to be thought of as such) dined if they could get a table. The headwaiter ran a very lucrative side business for a year or more before vexed and frustrated clients complained to the owner about his ripoffs.

The owner had no idea of the scam since he was too busy creating the wonderful food in the kitchen to know what his people out front were up to. To get a table in this "in scene," diners had to slip hundred-dollar bills to the waiter before he would take them to a table (and since this was Hollywood where stars are a dime a dozen he was not in any way impressed even when really big names came in looking for a burger and French fries). He must have grossed tens of thousands of dollars before being reported to the owner.

PADDED BILLS

Exchange regulations and controls can be extremely tight in certain countries because the government desires to use the country's foreign currency earnings with the greatest care and attention to political priorities. The penalties for breaches of these regulations can be severe—imprisonment for offenders, confiscation of property (and not just the bagful of dollars you were caught with), and heavy fines are among them. Many have been tempted to engage in illegal dodges to get around the problem.

For example, in some countries you can arrange to have payment made to you not in the form of cash but in real goods, which you then sell to recover your money. If you are unable to get paid in dollars in Ghana but can acquire good-quality cocoa against payment in cedis you can ship out the cocoa to the United States and sell it for hard currency. The fact that you have to pay CIF may mean you are taking a loss on the original amount owed to you, but in a choice between a loss and a total loss you don't really have a choice!

To obviate the cost of shipping real goods out you can try acquiring some high-value item that you can take with you, though here you run the risk of being stopped at customs and searched. Diamonds, gold, artifacts, and such are too obvious for even the dimmest customs official to miss (and by no means assume that customs officials in other countries are any less smart than they are in your own).

I know a negotiator who has avoided currency regulations for years by the simple expedient of using local currency to buy rare stamps which he sticks in his wallet and sells in London. Two things favor his choice of payment. He knows a rare stamp when he sees one, and, though he has been searched at customs several times, nobody has yet noticed his postage stamps!

But do watch the proposition that you should enhance the value of your invoice by 30 or more percent. This is often put to you by people who can get foreign currency to pay for their imports. They are using the scam of an invoice loaded in this way to build up personal foreign currency accounts abroad. You might be tempted to go along with this in order to get paid (he has an incentive in seeing that you are paid) because passing on the excess payment to your client's personal account costs you nothing.

The problem is that by massaging an invoice in this way you may not get paid at all because there is no way that a court is going to enforce an invoice that you issued with the intention, in the court's eyes, of avoiding their country's exchange controls.

To be convicted for this offense, even if you are safely out of the country, might draw the attention of your own country's authorities to your proclivities for slightly shady dealing.

So all those who have tipped a waiter for giving them a nice table (and there are always nicer tables than the one you have been shunted to) must accept that this petty ripoff is widespread throughout "civilization."

Politicians are often in the news when one of their esteemed number is forced to resign in clouds of corruption charges. The United States had a whole series of these unfortunate incidents in the 1970s, and an American vice-president resigned accused of accepting favors from constituents.

The fact remains, however, that even with the incidental examples of corruption in the United States, corruption here is nothing like on the scale that you will find in the Third World at all levels of society. If this raises for you deeply felt moral issues, you will have to overcome them some way or do your business elsewhere. Legislators pass laws against corruptly seeking business abroad, and moral leaders often make speeches condemning it, but the combined effect of laws and condemnation has not been sufficient to stem the practice.

Go-betweens

Open or thinly disguised corruption—paying off go-betweens for securing multimillion-dollar business—has proven to be vulnerable to inquiry and, if established, to prosecution in the home country of the business concerned (even if ignored in the country where the payoff for the order occurred). Hence, big business negotiators have become more subtle about disguising the bribes—known euphemistically as "commissions"—and they have become more careful to cover their tracks.

To use a go-between in itself indicates that you expect a commission will have to be paid, for no go-between (yet) has gotten business for an overseas company for nothing.

Some large corporations contribute to party funds in the country they do business in and in return, they are allowed special concessions to do their business. In Zimbabwe, for example, several major trading corporations have strong links with the government, and some have links with all the major political figures in the country. This is not necessarily a case of financial corruption; the firms concerned arrange mutually beneficial contacts for the Zimbabwe government abroad, do favors for government personnel in their official capacities, and make special donations to official activities without any implication that the individuals in government personally benefit from this relationship.

In sum, you will have to decide how you are going to cope with this problem. At the lowest level of getting into and around a country you will have to tip, bribe, dash, baksheesh, or commission those whose cooperation is necessary for you to function there. Once you cross that line (and be sure that you will have to do so), you will be faced with another and yet another as the sums at stake become progressively larger.

You can leave it to a go-between and let him deal with the

officials that need taking care of, or you can take care of them yourself. But be clear on this: There is no legal way to bribe somebody, and you are personally vulnerable once you attempt to do so.

Paying them in their own country out of the money for the deal is one way to settle up, but this leaves you exposed when you hand over the cash. Paying them through bank accounts abroad (the famous numbered Swiss account system) is as risky.

To set up a money deal with a Swiss bank on behalf of somebody else will involve your own staff, and you will then be vulnerable to their moods and sense of grievance in the future if something goes wrong with your relationship with them. (Many office romances that go sour end up with the boss in court on charges varying from income-tax evasion to bribery, so protect yourself from the same by *never* dating anyone on your own staff.)

Your go-between may promise undying loyalty and confidentiality to you and your company in accepting the bribe but, given the human rights records of many of these countries, you cannot be sure that he will remain so adamant in defense of your interests once handed over to the tender mercies of interrogators who do not recognize the Geneva Convention when they question prisoners, and have orders to find out who gave him the money, how much was given, and where the money is now.

Your next, innocent, visit to that country could be the prelude to some very uncomfortable experiences. (If you think Third World hotels have a long way to go before they are comfortable, you should compare them to their prisons!)

The bribery of tips

I have never heard anybody give satisfactory advice on how to cope with this problem in business and not just in the

Third World. There is a thin, almost transparent, line between a gift for goodwill and a gift as an inducement.

At Christmas in the United States firms send out sometimes lavish gifts to their clients. A case of whiskey is lavish in anybody's terms, and when it lands on the desk of a named individual who happens to be the buyer of your products, can you be sure that this is no more than a seasonal gesture of goodwill? Some companies, in an effort to prevent inducement of key personnel, insist that all gifts to clients be pooled and shared out among the entire staff. To get around this, some suppliers send their Christmas gifts to the home address of the person they wish to cultivate.

And what of taking potential clients to lunch? I have lost count of the lunches I have given or been given over the years, though I have never lost any sleep over the ethics involved. (I have lost sleep on occasion from the food and drink partaken of at these events!)

The giving and receiving of gifts is a delicate area in business, and only the circumstances and intentions of those involved can really determine on which side of the thin line gift-swapping falls.

When we receive exceptional service we often reward it in some way—a tip, a letter of commendation, a profuse thank-you—and in some places it pays to tip before you receive the service to make sure that you enjoy it.

To arrive empty-handed at a private home for dinner with a business associate can appear to be less than polite. Hence, many people go to some lengths to ensure that they arrive with some flowers, chocolates, perfume, or brandy for the lady or gentleman of the house. Others follow up an evening's socializing with a business partner with a small gift for the children.

In some countries there is an expectation that those whom you deal with will receive some gift, the nature and expense of the gift varying from one country to another. In the Philippines, gifts reflecting personal gratitude for favors received are on a scale unlikely to be accepted in other countries. Business partners, and those who wish to become so, can engage in swapping of gifts in the price range of 1,000 dollars plus without embarrassing each other. In Spain, gifts in the ball-point pen range are more likely to be acceptable.

Covering risks

Commercial risks can be insured against, and the extent of international trade ensures that insurance is a huge industry. Premiums are fixed for all kinds of transactions in all parts of the world, and where losses occur the losers can collect their insurance.

The insurance companies employ loss adjusters who travel the globe to assess the extent of the losses by claimants and where appropriate, to negotiate a settlement, sometimes with third parties. A friend of mine is a loss adjuster for a Lloyds syndicate, and he spends most of his time visiting West Africa, particularly Nigeria. He claims to be able to spot a fraudulent claim half a mile away and always delights in finding a way to reduce the net cost of a payout by an ingenious application of the principles of salvage of property. In one case he arranged for a burned-out factory (a case of arson) to be cleared inside where the roof had collapsed and turned into a walled parking lot for trucks. This reduced a total loss to a partial loss.

Insurance companies pay out when they receive legitimate claims, and they are prepared to pursue remedies through the courts when necessary, where they suspect fraud or other illegal acts. Much could be written about negotiating with insurance companies over claims. The most that can be said about the prospects of bettering insurance companies in negotiation can be summed up in the observation that insur-

NAIVETÉ IS NO DEFENSE

Many years ago when I had just started as a salesman I chanced upon what I thought was a great opportunity to make a large and relatively certain sale and in my enthusiasm, I did not take enough care to think through its legalities.

I had been discussing with a buyer the products I was selling—industrial spraying equipment—and after my sales pitch the conversation went on to nonbusiness matters. The buyer, a young man of my own age, had just passed his driving test and was very anxious to buy his first car. His problem was that he did not have the necessary deposit.

I went away but thought over the selling sequence, and the conversation about the buyer's desire for a car came back to mind. I was on a company car-purchase scheme. The monthly payments were made by my company out of my sales commissions, and I wondered if we could offer the buyer something similar.

I asked my boss if he had any objections as to who got the discount we were able to offer on our products and accessories. He said no, as long as we got the order, but wondered why I was asking since it was obvious that the customer got the discount.

I then explained what I intended to offer the young buyer. We would supply his company's spraying needs but at full list price. In return for the initial order we would put up the deposit on a new car for him. If he ensured that we would receive a regular monthly order for spares, paint, and hoses we would continue to pay the monthly payments on his car out of the discount we would normally have given his company for purchasing our products.

My boss said to go ahead. The buyer went for the deal immediately and was driving a new auto within a week of our receiving his first order (and as far as I know each side kept to the bargain over the next year—I left for a better-paying job shortly afterwards).

Some time later I was in conversation with other sales staff at a "Thank God It's Friday" seminar and retold the story, much to the horror of the senior salesmen. They quickly informed me that the entire proposition was illegal as it was tantamount to offering an inducement; that is, it was bribery. I was appalled at my stupidity and was only half restored to calmness when they told me the practice was prevalent in many badly managed companies. Naturally, I never did such a disreputable thing again!

ance executives, like bookies, seldom go broke and most of them are fairly well off.

If they get their premium levels right, then the cost of paying out on claims is more than covered by what they take in from people who are of a pessimistic disposition. (Bear in mind that the insurance company in quoting a premium is judging that the insured-against risk will not occur and the person seeking the insurance is saying that it will.)

To assist in promoting exports, the governments of many countries have established funds to supplement insurance coverage for those risks that a commercial insurance partnership will not cover. In effect, the government agency will back an exporter against the risk of default on payment caused by, say, a collapse of a country's credit system through war, revolution, or general mayhem. The charge for this is related to the agency's estimates of the risk. If faced with the prospect of a total loss the exporter can pay a premium and get covered for most of the cost of his exports. (This also helps sometimes to raise credit for his company.)

Errors of judgment, however, are still made. Firms can still take risks (thus saving on premium costs), or they may find themselves to be not sufficiently covered to be recompensed fully if a possible situation becomes a reality. When the timing of insurance coverage and its acceptance by those concerned is out of phase with commercial pressures to sign and be damned, there is always the real possibility that something will happen (Murphy's Law) before the paperwork is completed. At this point the exporter is on his own, and the losses could be crippling.

On getting paid

The next largest problem after that of the morality of paying "commissions" to smooth the path of doing profitable business is the simple, and ultimately more important, one of getting paid for your products. Securing business is only one aspect of staying in business. You have to get paid for what you deliver, and this can be a problem when dealing with clients a long way from the reach of your own courts. (It is sometimes difficult to get paid even when clients are just across the road from your local court.)

International trade would be inhibited greatly if some means had not been found to ensure that suppliers got paid by importers. There is much that can go wrong between an order being signed and the cash for the product arriving safely in your bank account.

In a society where commercial contracts are protected by the full force of the law there is always the remedy of suing somebody who has not paid for your products. This works more or less efficiently, but it is, or can be, very expensive to get justice. Winning a legal case may still leave you with losses if you cannot collect on the compensation.

Where the law is weak or heavily biased in favor of local people (not uncommon in parts of the world—your adversary's uncle may not only be his partner, he may also be the local magistrate!) recourse to lawyers may not be your best solution to a payment problem. Calling in the lawyers could set you back in your quest to be paid if the local businessman regards such action as an affront to his integrity.

Hence, whereas a detailed grasp of the intricacies of the

law of international contracts is a necessary attribute for the
international negotiator, it certainly is not sufficient by itself.
A good deal more is needed, much of it common sense and
some of it the result of hard-earned experience.

One of the most common ways of paying for goods is for
the buyer to open a letter of credit in favor of the seller. Negotiators have to watch the conditions that are attached to
such a letter—these are negotiable and as such should be var-
ied to suit your interests. A failure to do so in normal circumstances exposes you to serious risk of loss.

Ideally, you should require that you receive payment for
your goods without the option of the buyer having final say
on whether payment should be made in full and when he
should pay. To avoid buyer's discretion you will require that
the letter of credit be irrevocable in some way. When it is
due, providing you produce the agreed documentation (proof
that the goods have been sent or that they have arrived at the
buyer's premises), there will be no way for the bank to refuse
payment.

This should lead you to require that the irrevocable letter
of credit be confirmed and payable by a sound bank (that is,
one that can be trusted), preferably in your own country. If
you agree to conditional payments in any way (and you may
have to do so, depending on who needs the business the
most—though remember nobody needs business so badly that
they are prepared to do it for nothing) you might find that
your interpretation of what should trigger off a payment does
not conform to your opposite number's perception of the situation.

He can save himself some cash by holding onto money for
as long as possible, and if he has a cash flow problem anyway
he is more than likely to seek ways of taking credit with as
many suppliers as possible. Any discretion allowed in the letter of credit might prove to be too tempting for him not to
exercise it on one spurious ground or another.

The confirmed, irrevocable letter of credit with the most

stringent of payment conditions protects you. What about him? If he is in a position to require some commitment from you (and this is very likely to be the case since you have competitors in world markets) he will require you to agree to a performance bond of some kind.

Briefly, a performance bond requires you to pay to him a sum of money (usually a percentage of the value of the order in the letter of credit) if you breach some condition of delivery, such as timing, quality, or quantity. Unconditional performance bonds have become increasingly popular recently. Under these your bank must pay to the importer's bank a predetermined sum of money if he merely requests it. You have no defense in this last case, which is why these performance bonds are so popular with those traders who persuade suppliers to agree to them. No business is worth committing yourself to an unconditional performance bond, so, in a word, don't!

If you have agreed to an unconditional performance bond and he invokes it you are going to get less for your goods than you priced them at. Therefore you must ensure in your negotiations that your unconditional performance bond is unstoppable if, and only if, his letter of credit meets your terms of business; that is, it is confirmed, irrevocable, and paid through a sound bank. This does not remove the risk, it only minimizes the loss, but once again a loss is better than a total loss.

Having taken all possible precautions to make sure that you are paid you might still have problems in collecting some accounts. Credit control is an important subject in business management, and many a road to ruin for normally sound companies has begun by neglecting to run a sound credit control operation. I worked for six months once in the credit control department of a large expanding business (which, long after I left, went broke!). Negotiating skills are required in such an operation, and it ought not to be left to casual labor to run it.

Kinds of crooks

You may have to face the task of going out to visit a client to get your money (or as much of it as you can manage under the circumstances). This requires a lot of guts and determination. Debt collecting has never been one of civilization's most popular professions. Many people regard debt collectors as bullies in search of money.

In international business you cannot afford to be blasé about your debtors. Many countries, some with impeccable legal systems, can hide rogues and crooks in among traders who are genuinely in temporary trouble. Few countries in the Third World would qualify as having an impeccable legal system, and some that do (for example, India) have long since had their system so clogged up with bureaucracy and place seeking that justice has become a rare commodity and never swift.

Treating all debtors the same, irrespective of their individual and personal integrities, will tarnish your reputation (and may not get you your money). You have to visit the country and meet with the debtor to make your own judgments about the true reason for nonpayment of your invoices.

There are different types of crooked dealers: those who never intended to pay in the first place and who gave every sign of not doing so but you thought you were smart enough to beat them to the honey pot (in other words, you got greedy and took risks); those who intended to pay at first but got to like the idea of not paying as they got greedy (that is, you got lazy and took risks); and those who never intended to pay at all but assured you convincingly that they did (that is, you got soft and took risks).

Fortunately there is an antidote to these mistakes. It's called *experience*, and as you gain it you will know how to recognize the crooked dealers who ultimately don't pay from those traders who do. Unfortunately, it's almost impossible to separate the nonpayers from the payers in advance, so you will only know the difference after you get paid, or not, as the case may be. Therefore, you should assume that you are dealing with a nonpayer until the cash appears in your account (or bag if you have to go to collect it in person!).

For all kinds of reasons you may have accepted an order for your products that is not covered by a letter of credit of any kind or if it is, some technical problem has emerged not covered by what you thought was an irrevocable letter of credit.

The buyer agreed to pay you in due course, and he may have had every intention of so doing until something came up. You will have to decide whether to wait in the hope of getting your money, or to take what you can in final settlement, or simply *in ultimo extremis*, to write it off as a bad debt.

Do not underestimate the need for deciding upon the latter course. Far too many people can get emotionally attached to a debt problem and put time and resources into trying to collect a sum of money that are way beyond the potential economic gain from so doing ("It's not the amount, it's the principle"—to which the appropriate response is, "Sometimes it is necessary to rise above principle" and put your bad debt down to experience).

Some payment is better than none

Again, in debt situations, the broad principle applies that some payment is better than no payment. Getting them to agree to some payment could take some imaginative and creative thinking on your part, followed by some carefully controlled negotiating.

Here, the thing to remember is to concentrate on your proposed remedy and not on your grievance (that they have not paid). Harping on their failure to comply with the contract could irritate them to the point that they cease to concern themselves with your problems.

Threatening them with legal action, berating them for alleged failings, attacking their integrity, and publicly humiliating them in front of their peers are all routes to a useless deadlock. It is very easy for people to become nonavailable, and trying to find somebody in another country who does not want you to find them is more than you perhaps have time for. Get them to discuss with you your reasonable remedy for the problem, and you will get closer to a solution in a shorter period of time than by any other method.

What kinds of things could you propose? Only the limits of your imagination will exhaust the possibilities. You will not only be called upon to negotiate a settlement but also, more than likely, will have to supervise its implementation.

If they can't pay you for your machinery, how about paying you in kind with some of the output from the machines? If they cannot pay you for raw materials, how about paying you with some of the processed output? If they cannot pay you in hard currency, how about paying you in local currency to enable you to export some physical goods to sell elsewhere?

If they cannot pay 100 percent of the debt, how about a cash payment now for 65 percent in final settlement? If the firm to which you sent materials has gone broke before paying for the goods, how about their releasing your materials for removal from their premises in consideration of your dropping all claims on them? (If the owners won't or can't agree to this, how about—though it's risky and probably not legal—a small "commission" to the gatekeeper to let your trucks in during his lunch break?)

Collecting debts is a difficult and tiring job. It can also be dangerous. (Remember, most people love their enemies more than debt collectors.) I once accompanied a collector on a visit to one of the poorer Arab countries. After much negotiation and hassle, the Arab businessman agreed to make a settlement of 35,000 dollars cash against a paper debt of 90,000 dollars. The problem was that the negotiation was so full of menace that we were worried about getting to the airport safely without being robbed or even worse.

When we arrived later that afternoon to collect the cash we told the importer that we had just enough time to get to our hotel and collect our things before going out to the airport for the next flight home. The money was duly counted out slowly into a bag, and we signed the receipt and the agreement that this was a final settlement. We had asked his people to arrange a taxi to take us to our hotel. It duly arrived and we drove off in it in that direction.

Two blocks along we ordered the taxi to turn off the road and reverse direction toward the border, about ninety miles away, skipping the visit to our hotel and abandoning our possessions there (which were not worth much in value and were visible in the form of almost empty bags waiting for us at the front desk). We showed the driver a fistful of dollars and told him that if he made it to the border without stopping we would pay him a handsome fee.

This he did (and Arab drivers without doubt are the most hair-raising speed demons in the world; at times I was not sure whether we wouldn't have been safer facing our would-be attackers). When we got to the border (about the time our plane was leaving for London) we paid the driver 100 dollars in small bills, passed through customs thankfully without a hitch, and caught another taxi on the other side to that country's airport.

I have no idea whether our fears were justified, but am content in the knowledge that, being still alive, I have the luxury of speculating about it.

Fortunately, most of your business deals will be less dramatic, and you should, on the whole, manage to complete transactions without being menaced by wars and revolution and with payment in full for your trouble. But things do go wrong, and one sure cause of them doing so is your agreeing to sign something that you know in the cold light of day is not kosher. If you wish to avoid getting trapped into bad-debt situations, do not sign anything that can be to your disadvantage. No business is worth the ultimate hassle of risking your future, and that of your company, in pursuit of a marginal gain. If you need business so badly that you will take unusual, extraordinary, and large risks, then perhaps you ought not to be in that business at all.

ANSWERS TO SELF-ASSESSMENT TEST 9

1 **a** He could think you were impugning his character, and this could get you into more trouble (of the more than it's worth kind).   (**−10**)
b You are impugning his character, and you are now in deep trouble. (His four colleagues lounging by his jeep are itching to show you damn foreigners who's in charge of Ogoland now!)   (**−15**)
c Very good. You may now drive off unmolested—though you may not get your 50 quonks change.   (**10**)

2 **a** Your best bet, and if your client is genuine he should agree to something like this.   (**10**)
b Your caution is commendable, though it might be unrealistic. Insist on something like *a* if you must sign.   (**5**)
c It's always a bad move to agree to high-risk ventures that you cannot afford to lose on. If he calls up your performance bond it will cost you 23,000 dollars, no matter whether you have performed well or not. A sure road to ruin.   (**−10**)

3 **a** Hard-headed approach. It might not get you your money. Something is always better than nothing in the debt business.   (**0**)
b Poor response and it puts your company's 100,000 dollars at the mercy of the Indian legal system.   (**−10**)
c The best move initially. See for yourself and make a judgment (that's what being a manager is all about). If his story is true you could go on to try *d*; if not you go to *a*, with the threat of *b*.   (**10**)
d A step in the right direction, best after *c*.   (**5**)

SELF-ASSESSMENT TEST 10

1 You are in highly competitive negotiatons with an Indonesian government agency, and you suspect your rivals are desperate to get the business. You are approached one evening at your hotel by somebody who offers to sell you a copy of your rival's quotation. Do you:

a Ask how much?
b Say no?
c Call the police?

2 While you are negotiating a deal to develop an oil field, you are handed a file by your opposite number that contains the printouts of the well test borings done in the area by the exploration company. On taking these back to your hotel you find inside the file an unsealed envelope marked "confidential" and labeled clearly as a detailed proposal to develop the wells from your competitor, who you know is in the running for the contract. Do you:

a Open the envelope to read and copy the details?
b Keep the envelope closed?

3 Sanctions have been imposed on Ogoland by the United Nations, but by dint of your highly specialized knowledge you know of a way to supply Ogoland with consumer goods with small risk of detection and with a certainty of high profits. Do you:

a Approach the Ogoland government with details of your scheme and a cash contract to implement it?
b Decline to do so and instead approach your own government with a view to having the gap plugged that you have spotted?
c Approach somebody else who you know is sympathetic to Ogoland and offer to sell the scheme to him?

CHAPTER 10

Negotiating Close to the Wire—or, How Politics Inhibits Trading

The end of free trade

That free trade would be beneficial to all is one of those un-
doubted truths that have been central to economic theory
since Adam Smith. As Rousseau might have put it, trade is
better free, but everywhere it is in chains. How can this be?
It is largely because those who would fetter trade in some
way do so to gain more at somebody else's expense.

The problem with governments (recognized long ago by
Adam Smith) is that they listen to plausible but nevertheless
nonsensical demands for protection for some of their constituents, which are always dressed up as sacred expressions of
the "national interest" when in fact they are merely the special pleading of people who want to make a cosy living at the
consumers' expense.

Smith himself was pessimistic about the chances of the
British government in the 1770s following his advice to liber-
ate trade; it took more than sixty years before his recommendations were followed. Meanwhile, free trade principles
never really caught on anywhere else. By the early twentieth
century the world had swallowed one protectionist policy
after another. When the world succumbed to protectionism

227

in the 1930s the scene was set for the worst depression the capitalist world had seen, made far worse by the "export unemployment" policies of the world's major trading partners. At the end of World War II the major trading nations saw sense for a while and embarked on an ambitious program of eliminating tariff and nontariff barriers. While these momentous negotiations were under way they adopted a temporary measure known as the General Agreement on Tariffs and Trade (GATT).

Unfortunately, the special pleas of the far from undefeated proponents of protection within each country resulted in a very cautious approach to major reforms of world trade rules, and the temporary GATT provisions became permanent. This has meant a forty-year slow march through gradual reductions in tariffs (the so-called Dillon, Kennedy, and Tokyo rounds of negotiations) rather than a sudden bonfire of all the restrictions that exist in world trade.

The world is poorer as a result, or rather it is less rich than it could have been. Countries still have protected industries. These both force up the price that consumers pay for the goods producers insist on making within their own borders and oblige taxpayers to heavily subsidize such sunset industries (which consequently reduces the funds available for the nation's sunrise industries). Meanwhile, lower cost, often better quality, goods of the same type are available from foreign sources but are kept out by quotas and other restrictions or priced out by penal tariffs.

The delay in abandoning protection in all countries has led to renewed efforts to reinstitute even stiffer protection to cope with the problems brought about by the current world recession. Fortunately, this drive to rebuild the ruinous protectionism of the 1930s depression has been held back—though not entirely defeated—by memories of that previous protectionism which undoubtedly worsened and prolonged the Great Depression.

How long this flimsy barrier to protectionism will continue depends on how long the current depression continues, and we must be pessimistic when we note the rousing cries for protectionism articulated by political candidates and parties recently.

Thus, those of you who embark on a career of exporting your company's products, in competition with other foreign companies and those that are located within the importing country, must face up to the fact that free trade is not a fact of business life and that governments in overseas countries at least replicate the restrictive trade practices of your own country and probably add a few other obstructions as well.

Government restrictions

We do not have space to go into a comprehensive discussion of all the restrictions imposed on trade by governments throughout the world, and anyway that is not my purpose in raising the issue. What I want to convey to you is a feeling for the restrictive environment in which your exporting and importing activities will have to operate.

Governments are sovereign powers within their territories and jealously guard their authority. As a foreigner you have limited rights, and one of them does not include the privilege of ignoring the regulations laid down by the government of the territory that you wish to trade in.

There are several ways in which you can do business with the people of another country.

You can export your goods direct to the country using whatever transport is convenient. Some countries might require you to use their national shipping lines or airlines and not go into the free market looking for the best deal.

When your goods get to the borders of the country concerned they will have to have appropriate documentation

TRAGEDY AT MAKOLA

Ghana's economy has been going through a bad time and a recent collapse in economic confidence led to a military coup. The military had good intentions but remained economically illiterate. Faced with serious food shortages and rapidly rising prices they chose the age-old method of intervention. This never works.

They sought popularity by blaming the shortages on black-market stockpiling; they took stern measures against smuggling; they instituted price controls; and finally they turned the mob on the market traders in Makola (in Accra). The mob destroyed the market by fire, violently dispersed the market "mammies," and still went home hungry.

By intimidating the only people who could be mobilized to get food into Ghana—not by exhortation but by self-interest—the government perpetuated the shortages. If it had told the market mammies that they could keep all their profits from trade, if they had repealed all laws against smuggling, and if they had abandoned price controls—in other words done the exact opposite of what they did—they would now be ruling a fitter, fatter, and well-fed Ghana.

Why? Because it is a law of human nature that if you make it worth some people's while to put themselves out they will always do so, and if by doing so they bring food into a starving country they will do more good for the people than any other group. Next door to Ghana, the Ivory Coast has none of Ghana's draconian laws about food prices. It is also suffering none of Ghana's self-inflicted ailments.

correctly filled in and duly stamped with approvals, often from more than one source within the government's apparatus. They might have to meet various restrictive criteria regarding quotas, quality, noninfestation, or no inputs from embargoed third parties—as in the Arab boycott of Israel, for example.

Your goods may have to wait at the entry port while they are "inspected" by government officials or be taken at your expense to some obscure place for the same. The French did this with Japanese video recorders for a while, in retaliation for the often prolonged "inspections" required by Japanese law before imports can be distributed in Japan.

Once they are released you should be able to distribute them in the country for sale, but other restrictions may apply here. For instance, you may not be permitted to sell the goods directly to consumers or might not be able to do so because the entire distribution network is a closed business for foreigners, as it is in Japan and, effectively, in Scandinavia, and particularly in Finland. You might have to enter into some kind of agency agreement with a local company.

Agency agreements are required in most Arab countries, and many others require at least partnership status for their nationals. Brazil has heavy restrictions on direct imports through a licensing arrangement. This effectively forces would-be exporters to Brazil into partnership in joint ventures with local firms.

You will have to find a suitable local national or company with which to do business before you send off the first consignment. This can be a hit-or-miss affair. Not every business in the world is automatically compatible with others and though the contacts you make might at first appear to be with people of sound mind, bank balance, and body, events could demonstrate your fallibility in picking winners. Getting out of a joint venture that you ventured into as an adventure could prove to be more difficult than you expected.

When you are dealing in projects worth many millions of dollars, you need not be dealing just with a local company. The government of the territory could very well be in charge of the proposal, if not the negotiations, and this would add a round of complications to the purely business aspects of the deal. Governments are run by politicians, and politicians face numerous pressures, some of them totally antithetical to the interests of commerce and trade. The civil servants whom you negotiate with could be under instructions from their political masters to introduce into the deal terms and conditions

IF IT'S FOOD, STALL IT

A Third World country was in dire need of emergency food supplies, and the United States decided to ship out its spare grain to help feed the famine area.

A shipping line quoted fifteen dollars a ton to ship the food to the country. The journey required about three weeks in all because of the distance between the ports.

When the ships arrived off the coast they had to off-load into lighters to get the food into the warehouses on shore. The local lighter owners charged fifteen dollars a ton to ship the grain over a distance of 450 yards to the warehouses.

On the next trip, four weeks later, the company's ships had to wait to off-load because the warehouses were still full of grain from the previous trip. The grain had not been moved inland to the famine areas because of delays at customs in clearing the grain for import. This was of no direct concern to the shipping company as they were paid demurrage for every ton they delivered that stayed within the port area.

Nevertheless, the shipping managers thought the whole episode reflected badly on the governments involved in the deal. Old hands thought this was typical of the famine business, which in their view (perhaps more than a trifle cynical) was only an excuse for the politicians to feel good about fixing a relief operation, with attendant publicity, without anybody following up on the actual deliveries to those who badly needed them. The local customs guys were only doing their jobs and were not concerned with the wider issues of why the excess grain imports were needed in the first place—nobody from the central government apparently had informed them.

wholly unnecessary to its commercial success and perhaps worse, directly contrary to profitability.

Where governments have set up procedures to process business proposals between foreigners and nationals you can bet your next bottle of Chianti that these procedures take time to go through, if only because of the heavy demands upon the personnel inflicting them on an increasing number of would-be traders. This, of course, opens up opportunities for greased line jumping, which serves to prolong the procedures even more for those without the grease.

Goods in—money out

All of the above arrangements only get your goods (perhaps) to the country itself. You still have to get your money out, and here an entire battery of exchange control regulations awaits you like an obstacle course for determined commandos. The remittance of profits is always contentious, and it's no different with the remittance of income.

Your getting paid is not determined by the normal rule of business—somebody who buys your products must pay for them—for it depends greatly on the economic policies and circumstances of the country with whom you would trade. You can check the payment status of a country with the international division of your bank.

Given that getting paid by your own government can take time, you ought not to expect too much in the way of haste from a foreign government. The slowness of the U.S. government to pay its bills is notorious among contractors—it's the largest single complaint in surveys—and many overseas governments have adopted similar administrative systems for running their affairs. If these delays are likely to cripple you, and they can last for a year or more, you had better review your need to do business with these governments.

Thus, government restrictions and interventions in trade between their nationals and you are of considerable significance, and you must take a realistic look at them before embarking on a trading venture abroad. In one sense this is the purpose behind some of the restrictions—to deter trade—and the purpose behind the rest of the restrictions is to control trade. Both purposes are served by the mountains of paper that govern trade between countries, and you must be familiar with them if you wish to survive commercially.

Political restrictions

If the normal restrictions discussed above were all that you had to worry about that would be bad enough, but there is another layer of restrictions imposed on world trade, which has a more political purpose behind it than simply deterring or controlling trade for economic reasons. I refer to the various sanctions and embargoes that operate around the world.

For example, members of the North Atlantic Treaty Organization operate a trade embargo on the export of certain goods to countries of the Soviet bloc through the Co-ordinating Committee on Export Controls (COCOM). This economic embargo is aimed at preventing war materials, or materials that could be used in a military role, from being exported from the technologically advanced Western countries to what is regarded as a potential enemy alliance (the Warsaw Pact or WARPAC).

Items on the COCOM lists cover the obvious ones of munitions and military equipment, and atomic energy materials and plants, plus a long list of items under an "industrial and commercial" category. It is this last list that creates the most controversy between companies in NATO and their respective governments (who administer COCOM regulations). To remove an export item from any of the lists (and there are about 150 items on the industrial and commercial list) requires the unanimous consent of all the NATO members in principle, but since each government is responsible for its interpretation of whether an item qualifies for the list or not, there is always a side controversy going on as one government approves an item while another does not.

All your trade with Eastern bloc countries, including China, must meet the COCOM regulations. This adds yet another round of complications to your negotiations with the authorities in these countries (discussed in chapters 3 and 7), so you had better make sure you are only committed to the deal if you can get export clearance from the U.S. government and COCOM.

Another level of politically motivated trade restrictions concerns the sanctions and embargoes on specific countries. The Arab states, for example, embargo any company trading with them from also trading with Israel. They include a clause in their contracts requiring you to agree that you support the Arab boycott of Israel, and if you do not sign this clause you do not get the business unless you are big enough, like the United States government, to refuse—the Saudis want U.S. military equipment more than they want U.S. signatures in support of the boycott.

How you handle this demand is a policy problem, not a negotiating issue. Of course, the imposition of the clause in practice may be less thorough than the clause suggests. But, as I have noted, the Arabs do not admit you to their countries if your passport has an Israeli visa or evidence that you have visited or are about to visit Israel in it. You must carry two passports in this case. Open flouting of the boycott could be enough to have you blacklisted, but covert and unpublicized trade with Israel might be tolerated (unless it is in military equipment or in materials destined for the occupied territories).

You need not take any political boycott as absolute. There

is evidence, typically of a kind that is difficult to prove, that even Arab states will trade with Israel under certain circumstances. (There is an old Israeli joke about the enmity between the Arabs and the Jews which has one Israeli asking another why the Arabs insist on having so little to do with them. "Why do they insist on paying retail when they could get it wholesale?")

There is always constant pressure to impose sanctions on South Africa. These already exist in respect to military equipment, especially equipment that could be used internally. But the fact is that South Africa's neighbors, out of sheer economic necessity, do trade with it in a whole range of commodities and would themselves be severely damaged if sanctions were imposed on them by the rest of the world.

Economic sanctions have a very poor record of political success, though this does not stop them being imposed from time to time. If your company happens to be caught in the middle of a sanctions war you need not necessarily write off your business.

Sanctions were imposed on Italy before World War II for its invasion of Ethiopia. The Soviet Union promptly stepped in and supplied Italy with the oil that was being withheld by member states of the League of Nations.

The sanctions imposed on Rhodesia (now Zimbabwe) during "UDI" (Unilateral Declaration of Independence) were notorious for their ineffectiveness. If anything, the range and availability of imported goods in Rhodesia during the height of the sanctions were greater than they are in Zimbabwe now that the war has ended. South Africa refused to apply sanctions against its northern neighbor for political reasons, and most companies within the member states of the United Nations arranged their affairs so that their South African subsidiaries diverted goods northwards. The classic case was the oil embargo on Rhodesia through the Beira pipeline (which Lonrho owned and had to close down). Independent tankers

THE "ONLY FIVE MINUTES MORE" CLUB

During the 1970s, international business negotiators regaled each other with tales (some of which must have been sheer fantasy) of the five mile high club. Apparently, you joined this informal club if you participated in sexual relations while flying at over 30,000 feet (obviously in a 747 or DC10—surely only these aircraft have room for such shenanigans?).

I have always thought that such a "club" must be fairly exclusive. I was discussing the same with an American in a bar in Georgetown in Washington, D.C. when he told me about another, even more exclusive, club, but this was one that I was not in a hurry to join.

He said he was a founding member of the "only five minutes more" club. I asked him to explain.

"Well, it's like this," he said. "I was in the last plane out of Phnom Penh, Cambodia, and only five minutes more on the runway and we would have been learning Vietnamese."

I asked him what he was doing there, and he said, without the slightest blush, "Trying to lift out three Cambodian families for half a million dollars in diamonds. Unfortunately, I had to leave two families on the runway, and they had the diamonds! I regret the diamonds because that was my means of paying off the pilot—he nearly crashed the plane when he heard what I had left behind but, between his anger and the Vietnamese, I think I was right to get the hell out of there at the precise moment when I did, even if I had to leave a fortune behind doing so."

The nearest I have gotten to the only five minutes more club was catching a plane out of Beirut during one of their outbreaks of civil violence, and I can say in all honesty that that is the closest I ever want to be to qualifying for membership. In the meantime I'm still hoping to qualify for the much safer five mile high club!

simply supplied Rhodesia through ports in Mozambique and South Africa.

Sanction busting

Sanction busting is a lucrative business, and it is likely to undermine any politically motivated interference in trade apart from the prospects of other governments refusing to go along with the sanctions war, such as the Soviet Union and South Africa.

When a country is under sanctions pressure, it is open to proposals to supply it with what it needs. It is also generally willing to pay a high premium for those supplies, and this alone is sufficient to attract maverick and cowboy operators. Whenever a country is in trouble of this kind, especially during a war, its downtown hotels are full of opportunists offering deals to government officials to supply this or that on a grand scale.

During the Falklands war, the world was scoured by, or on behalf of, the Argentinians for military supplies, and some items reportedly were secured from French, South African, and Israeli sources.

The same has been happening in Iran over the past two years. Tehran has had its share of traders offering deals in military supplies for its army and air force and reportedly, the Israelis, through third and fourth parties, have been lending a judicious hand in some deals, on the principle that the enemy of my enemy (Iraq) is worthy of some support.

Should you go in for this business? Not if you are of a nervous disposition. When the world sees a pot of honey, the place near it gets crowded, and not all of those offering deals and megadeals are in a position to deliver anything like what they promise. This imposes on the government's negotiators the onerous task of sorting out the liars from the rest.

Opportunists, merchants of fantasies, timewasters, deluded crooks, con men, and enemy agents form a flood outside the doors of government officials who have money to burn and not a lot of time to get what they need. In the rush to sort things out, the officials can take arbitrary action against individuals in order to discourage all but the most genuine and serious suppliers.

The salutary example of somebody they believe is a time-wasting con man being badly maimed, or worse, has the effect of emptying the corridors as fast as they filled up. If you are a serious trader and have the resources to organize an operation on this scale, and can take the strain of running what is often a strictly illegal, and certainly an embarrassing, activity, you could make a financial killing.

If you are not troubled by your conscience, you have no reason not to engage in this business. Indeed, your government may be neutral in respect to the political issues at stake. While not giving you any blessing, they may not try to do anything to stop you, either. (For example, the weekly flights from Stansted airport, England, to Uganda during Amin's reign of terror were not illegal in Britain and were not stopped.)

But the basic rules of trade still apply, only more so: get paid in cash close to delivery, and upfront if possible, and keep your promises even if the side you are supporting is losing.

I know a guy who forgot this last part and thought he had gotten away with it when the government was overthrown, only to find he was being pursued by the former officials, now exiles, who wanted "their" money back and were prepared to kill him if they couldn't get it. Sensible man, he gave it back and went off to look for some less risky way to get rich.

A European politician, now dead, was a "treasurer" for a revolutionary movement in the Third World which eventually came to power. He died, and the money—many tens of thousands of dollars in foreign currency—apparently disappeared. The government concerned has still not given up trying to find it or punish the persons responsible; in fact, one man they caught up with was shot in Madrid some years back.

So if you fly out to Ogoland with a brilliant scheme to help a beleaguered government get the things it needs badly, you know the risks and rewards. You ought to ensure that they are reflected in your opening negotiating position, which, if the circumstances are desperate enough, might be closer to what you agree on than you would otherwise expect it to be.

Dirty tricks

Competition selects the winners and in doing so also selects the losers. Not everybody approaches losing with the same philosophical acceptance as you or I do, and we must therefore be aware of the pressures on those who don't like losing to try to do something to improve their chances.

The world of business is populated with people, and people in business are like people in most other walks of life. They are susceptible to gossip, rumor, innuendo, and outright deceit. This fact gives your rivals a potential lifeline if they are feeling pessimistic about their chances of getting the deal. They can blacken you in the eyes of your potential clients.

The use of dirty tricks in the search for business is legendary across the whole world. It is not confined to people in dirty raincoats selling dubious postcards and video nasties. Complaints about the use of dirty tricks have emanated from some of the most prestigious of boardrooms, though naturally what constitutes a dirty trick depends very much on the perception of the victim.

You will hear negotiators complain that their rivals cut

their prices to get the business, which seems to me to be unfortunate more than unfair. Some time ago when a British shipyard lost an order to a Finnish yard, it complained that, by its calculations, the Finns could not even pay for the materials for the ship for the price they were quoting, and therefore the government must be subsidizing the deal. The Finns replied that nothing was subsidized and challenged the British to prove their claim. The row went on for a while, but the feeling that there was something underhand going on persisted, though no evidence was forthcoming to establish this.

Preemptive "underhand" moves are likely to be justified on the grounds that if they are not undertaken the result will be that the business will go to a rival, who is suspected of being willing to sink to underhand moves anyway!

I am not going to discuss the lunacy of price cutting as a way of securing business, as I have fully dealt with that elsewhere (in *Everything Is Negotiable!*) and I do not think that such methods, in the dirty tricks sense, are really underhand, only stupid. Dirty tricks include two major techniques: bad-mouthing you and your company to potential or current clients (which stops you getting or keeping the business); and unauthorized access to information about your negotiating position or business operation (which enables a rival to pitch his deal in a more attractive and devastatingly competitive way).

In foreign trade you are doubly exposed to dirty tricks, if only because of the distances between you and your customers. In your absence your rivals can be in contact with your client's personnel, and by dint of charm, plausibility, and outright lying, inculcate them with a picture of you and your operation that is at variance with the facts.

It is common in business to find individuals in any company more disposed to one supplier than to another. Each supplier has its supporters and detractors in a client organization and like anybody else where something is at stake, you have to pay attention to your constituency. It does not take much to knock you out of the running. If you neglect your supporters by failing to visit the country enough times to be on hand to support them supporting you or by visibly letting the client down in some way with deliveries, quality, or spares, your rivals will use these incidents in the constant propaganda war against you.

A single failure could let them in the door on a trial basis, and you could be out the door for good or at least have to share the business with somebody else. Hence, visit your clients regularly and maintain contact with them in between through letters, telexes, and telephone calls. Get your people to back up your hard-won negotiated deal with an all-levels approach to communicating with all levels in the client's organization. Thus, when your rivals turn up and try to turn them against you, the initial defense of good (because they are regular) personal relations between your people and the client's should keep them off. At the very least you will get an early warning of any moves by rivals in this area, because you can be sure that their people will tell yours about what was said.

How about the dirty trick of industrial and commercial espionage? Here again you have a problem when you are negotiating abroad. You are a long way from home, and you are forced to use insecure communications to refer matters back or to get some guidance on a new issue.

Look at the issue of security. The clerk in the postal department may have been paid by the opposition to open and copy your correspondence, complete with price quotes and specifications. Nor can you be sure that your client's filing cabinets are immune to similar intrusions. There is not a lot that you can do about this, though you can refrain from using your client's mail room to send messages home. Use the local post office instead and avoid using hotel mail services.

Your own communications to your home base and the security arrangements there are within your control, up to a point. Those companies that engage in proper security procedures for sensitive commercial information are better placed to ensure some immunity from dirty tricks than those that are completely lax.

If what you have is worth stealing, somebody somewhere will endeavor to steal it. So you should take simple precautions to keep your valuables (in this case your information) to yourself.

Negotiators who have to report everything back while abroad are more vulnerable to having their information intercepted. Someone may be listening in on an extension, bugging the hotel telephone, copying your telex messages, photocopying your price lists, conditions, and other papers left in "safe" places, and so on. It is better to give long-distance negotiators as much authority to settle as possible and allow them to minimize home calls for guidance.

For convenience, negotiators often carry with them vast amounts of information, only a proportion of which is needed for a particular negotiation. For example, a company price list and procedures manual will contain materials relevant both to domestic and international business, and yet only one or two pages may be relevant to the particular deal being negotiated. If this information is gotten hold of by an unauthorized person, then the damage to you is extended way beyond the specific negotiations that you are in the country for. A simple stripping out of all unnecessary material from your file before you leave will minimize this damage. (It will also give you less to carry.)

A similar reason justifies my caution in chapter 2 not to take with you large amounts of office work unconnected with the negotiations at hand, with the intention (rarely realized) of doing some of it while traveling. Not only is it additional weight to carry, but it is vulnerable to a lapse in security.

In sum, you should support your overseas negotiation on a

"need to know" basis and select the materials that are to accompany the negotiator on a "need to go" basis. The negotiator should be made responsible for the security of the company's commercial information and should be required to demonstrate the measures taken to protect that information while he or she is abroad.

What happens if you come across commercially sensitive information regarding a rival? That would depend on how you came across it. If you have stolen it or engaged in some illegal acquisition of it, you are obviously in breach of the law and risk criminal charges. If, however, you come across it fortuitously, I can see no reason why you should not use that information, if only by sending it to your home base. Your rivals should be more careful with their secrets.

A negotiator I know was engaged in detailed discussions with an overseas client. He returned to his hotel and unpacked his briefcase to work on his figures and found a set of papers included in some material given to him by the client, which were his rival's quotation. He dithered for some time about this and decided to hand them back the next morning (having not dithered over reading them!). This he did, to the obvious embarrassment of his client. He did not get the business and has long wondered whether the client disbelieved his story that he acquired the papers accidentally and decided not to do business with a "spy."

Many negotiators acquire a facility for reading, upside down, the papers in front of their opposite numbers. Quite a few negotiators do pencil in their negotiating positions, especially figures, and these can be seen across a table. It is, of course, a silly thing to do—to pencil in your price limits like that—and the remedy is in your hands. Also, if you leave the room with your sensitive papers on the desk, you must expect your opposite number to lean forward and read them, and he must assume that this is what you intended him to do.

ANSWERS TO SELF-ASSESSMENT TEST 10

1 a I suppose you could claim that you were only trying to find out the price of the goods and still claim perfect integrity, though I suspect that you are fairly determined to let nothing stand in your way. You should go far in this rough-and-tumble business. **(10)**
b Surely you are someone of impeccable integrity who does not fear losing. May you never go hungry and may all your deals be profitable. **(10)**
c A trifle harsh, don't you think, to squeal on a guy who is not harming you? (Unless he gets to your papers!) If you feel that way, why not stick to *b*? Otherwise I might think you are a trifle self-righteous.
(10)

(All these answers score the same because there is no way to rank the ethical positions of others.)

2 a This is probably what most of us would do. If one acquires something by accident I see no ethical reason for not reading it, though I am not so sure about copying it! **(10)**
b You may feel good about this self-denial, but I suspect that nobody would believe you didn't open it. You gain nothing from not doing so. **(3)**

3 a Why not? I suppose it depends on how you feel about the reasons for the sanctions. The UN can be more than hypocritical in what it condemns and condones. You had better be sure, though, that you have a serious scheme and do not waste the time of Ogoland officials, as they might make an example of you. **(10)**
b Only the most pressing of humanitarian reasons would incline me to follow this line. The fact that you are prepared to do so without knowing why the sanctions have been imposed indicates a less-than-free-trade attitude to business. Perhaps you are a career civil servant? **(−10)**
c Nice one. It manages to be acceptable to one's own ideas about ethics and also make a profit out of somebody else's. It could get you the Gold Star of Ogoland with Oak Leaf Clusters as well as a couple of thousand dollars. **(10)**

CHAPTER 11

The Long-distance Negotiator—or, A Salute to Those Who Go Out and Get the Business

What's it all about?

This final chapter is a short salutation to the men and women who go out at all times of the year and get the business that the United States depends upon. Without exports we could not pay for our imports, and without imports we would be both poorer and at the mercy of overprotected domestic producers who know (and they all do!) how to take advantage of a lack of international competition.

Undertaking business abroad is no easy task. It takes a special breed of executive who is willing to fly off (often at very short notice) to a distant land and negotiate on behalf of his or her company, many employees of which care little about what is being done in their name and know even less about what is involved in doing it.

Faraway places, like green fields, can look very attractive at a distance. Go through the hassle of getting there and of functioning in what is for you, after all, a strange environment, and you begin to appreciate the kind of job that keeps you close to your hearth.

This is not to say that international business negotiators are all tired, worn-out, and boring. I met a fresh-faced lass only last month who was simply oozing with enthusiasm for her new job as an international representative for a designer clothing company. She was on one of those round-robin trips that take in a handful of European capitals in five days (naturally I refrained from advising her where to stay in each capital!), and she was tremendously keyed up to go out and get the job done. I admired her enthusiasm, though I could not share it as I was returning from a particularly grueling sixteen-hour-day speaking tour for a client in Sweden.

There is no doubt that the international negotiator is one of the great unsung heroes of modern times. As world trade increases, the role of the international negotiator is growing commensurate with the job in hand. Goods do not sell themselves—would that they could!—and it takes hard work in many different environments to get the business to keep the goods flowing from one country to the next.

In international business many are called and few are chosen, but still hundreds and thousands of new faces join the ranks each year. They try their best to extend their company's business or hold on to what it has already. Those that fall by the wayside are the necessary casualties in a continuous striving for business deals the world over; those that persevere deserve their material rewards, for they certainly do not acquire them easily.

Visit any airport

International negotiating requires travel, and travel soaks up energies as surely as any sport; only in travel the strain is prolonged over longer periods.

At any international airport you will see scores of negotiators embarking or disembarking, or more likely waiting in between flights, all carrying with them the hopes and the futures of their companies. What these men and women do when they get to where they are going can determine whether there is a company to come back to, or one worth making long-term plans for.

You can tell the negotiators from the tourists. Negotiators travel more often to more places, and consequently they are more at home in the complex tangle of an airport. They move about with an air of certain purpose about them rather than fidgeting their way from the indicator board to the gates.

The smarter negotiators seldom have too much luggage with them (tourists always have too much of everything, except patience), and they are organized for their flight. If they are in company they form a merry band, swapping stories of their last deals and their hopes for the next. In this sense, they are like sales staff the world over who regale each other with tales, jokes, and mutual "atrocity" stories of this or that dealer they all know—when, that is, they are not slamming into the reputations of their colleagues in other functions who don't understand anything about how tough it is out in the field.

There is a camaraderie among international business negotiators, partly expressing their competence and their pride in their work and partly their inner tensions about the next deal that they must tackle. True, some of them (all of them at one time or another!) talk up the deals they have negotiated—a little exaggeration here and there is surely as par for the course among negotiators as it is among those who would catch fish by rod and line. Mostly these little peccadilloes are harmless slips of personal integrity and are mostly caused by the need to appear worthy of one's trade in a world where it is not always sensible to go into the details of a private commercial deal.

When you next sit in an airport lounge—for, be sure, if you travel at all by air you will sit in some lounge for some time, perhaps for longer than you had planned—look around at your fellow travelers. Having separated out the tourists, check over the others. Most of these will be traveling on business. If you count them you will be surprised at just how many men and women fly for this reason only.

You will spot the first-timers, nervously checking and rechecking their tickets, always willing for someone to talk to them so that they can confirm their status and appear more confident than they feel. The old-timers will probably be pretending to be totally relaxed, even dozing to prove it, though their ears will be well attuned to departure announcements through the deepest of catnaps. Their faces will show the years, in some cases better than others, but the lines will be worn with the pride of experience. Their bags will show their experience as well—they will be working bags, a trifle battered but everywhere serviceable in every condition they might encounter. No smart Sunday-supplement luggage sets for negotiators!

Between the new and the retiring come the vast mass of business negotiators, in all shapes and sizes, all temperaments and moods, waiting for the takeoff like marines in a landing craft on D day. Those who want to talk and socialize will—it is from this band that you get all the advice on where to stay and what to do about foreign exchange ripoffs—and those who want to travel in solitude and contemplation will try to do so, either by physically slinking away crabwise from the hearty souls looking for a foursome for a bridge game from Houston to Bahrain (or just somebody with whom to drink their duty-frees) or immersing themselves in large paperbacks.

I know one guy who in search of solitude prominently displays around him a couple of issues of *The Watchtower*, a Jehovah's Witnesses newspaper, because nobody but nobody wishes to get into a long conversation all the way to Tokyo with somebody they think is a religious proselytizer!

Ten good rules for negotiating for business anywhere

The best of the breed of international business negotiators have several things in common. Observe them at work, imitate them, improve upon what you learn, and you will join their ranks.

First, you must get used to the idea of being a foreigner. There is no substitute for the acquisition of a little national humility. You don't have to go overboard the other way and renounce your birthright, but you must accept your place as a foreigner in the order of things. This means above all accepting that the world neither owes the United States a living nor necessarily owes it a good turn. What you get from your negotiating partners will depend on how much they think they need what you are offering, and if they can get a better deal elsewhere they should and will take it.

Second, you must get yourself organized for international business travel. Those who want to be the most successful negotiators fly first class, stay in good-quality hotels, take with them only that which they need, do not regard a long flight as an excuse for a boozy party, and are sensible about the very real problems of jet lag (they only go to bed in other time zones when it is time to do so there, not when they feel like it on arrival).

Third, you must learn something about the manners and customs of the people with whom you want to do business. You should not assume that anything that is quite acceptable in our culture is necessarily acceptable in all other cultures. One way to improve your acceptability as an international negotiator is to learn a little of the language of the people with whom you deal.

This advice also applies to those countries where the people speak a language akin to your own. For example, British and Australian negotiators speak a recognizable form of American English, but you would be foolish to leave it at that when you go to their countries to negotiate. The English-speaking peoples are separated by a common language, and you would be well advised to bone up on the local slang, dialect, and manners if you want to do business with your "cousins."

If you have any doubts on this score, think about the difference in approach within the tiny British Isles between the English and the Scots, and then consider how different the Australians have become from both the English and Scots over the years of separation.

When you are dealing with non-English-speaking peoples the advice is the same, only more so. Japanese manners and courtesies are entirely different from those of the Midwest of the United States. Fortunately, once you observe them you can adjust without too much discomfort to your sense of what is right or wrong—though a Japanese bath might be a tiny surprise the first time!

Fourth, you must adjust the pace of your negotiating to that of the people with whom you are trying to do business (they might have to do the same if they visit you in your country). It is no good trying to do anything much in a hurry, and it is absolutely hopeless to expect to be able to speed them up just because Father Time is knocking on your schedules.

In most parts of the world you will have to slow down, and it does not matter whether the delays are caused by bureaucratic procedures (as in the Soviet Union) or by the way they make decisions (as in Japan and the Middle East). Have patience, take longer, and don't give yourself unrealistic schedules.

Fifth, you must develop those skills of negotiating that are the same the world over. Begin with preparation (or knowing your own business better than your rivals). You must also know how to listen, react to what you hear, make conditional propositions ("If—then perhaps—"), repackage creatively, and bargain using conditional, and only conditional, offers ("If—then—").

Sixth, you must always remember that in a negotiation with anybody anywhere you always have the option of saying no to a deal that is in any way suspect, whether your suspicions concern the contract they want you to sign, the terms they want you to agree to, or the business ethics they want you to abandon.

You do not need to sign anything that does not meet your best and long-term interests. If you do sign something you ought not to have, then you will have to live with it (or without it).

This is all the more true when you have been working hard for a long time to get some kind of deal. You must adopt the attitude that bygones are bygones and previous investment in time and energy can never be recouped. Certainly you must never try to recoup them by agreeing to something that is not strictly what you can live with.

Hence, if Soviet negotiators want you to take goods in place of cash, or Germans want you to accept penalty clauses on delivery commitments, or Chinese negotiators want you to cut your prices on a "sell cheap, get famous" promise, or Australians want your goods on a consignment-only basis, or South Americans want exclusive agency rights, or Arabs want 15 percent commission, or Ogolanders want side-payments in a numbered Swiss account, or whatever (and there will be many "whatevers"!), you should always remember that although you have the authority to say yes, you also have the responsibility for what you say yes to. So, perhaps you should say no a little more often.

Seventh, you must cultivate the habit (until it requires no effort whatsoever) of never getting involved in discussions or comments upon any country's politics, religion, way of life, ethics of doing business, racial mix, legal processes, constitutional arrangements, methods of selecting its leaders, public or private morality, prevalence of tips, bribery and corruption, modes of dress or undress, laws regarding your personal preferences in sex, booze, drugs and porno videos, press freedom, or citizens' rights.

If you wish to combine a business career with reform of other countries you should reconsider your personal prospects. The internal affairs of other countries are none of your damn business, and in many parts of the world they do not take kindly to, or treat lightly, interfering visitors who forget what their visas say they are there for.

Your wonderful views on American-style democracy, feminism, the free market, income distribution, social welfare, local wars, racial strife, the treatment of offenders, and such should be left at home. If in your case that is not possible, then you should stay at home too!

Eighth, you must treat everybody with whom you deal with the greatest of personal respect, no matter how you feel about the way the negotiation is being handled. This applies to personnel on your own side as well as on the other side (even if you feel some of your people seem to be working for them!). Respect for the individual in business life is always a rare treat if you are on the receiving end of it and for that reason alone, it is well worth adopting as a policy in your own behavior toward others.

No matter how new and strange to you any culture in the world is, and no matter how intricate are the social obligations of the people you deal with, you can be sure of being accepted anywhere, in spite of any courtesy gaffes you make out of your ignorance or forgetfulness, if you display constant evidence of your respect for your opposite number as a person. There are no parts or peoples of the world where you will find exceptions to this principle; everybody reacts more warmly to those who they can see respect them than they do to those who they suspect do not.

Ninth, you must always endeavor to the best of your ability—and sometimes beyond that—to meet the terms of the contracts you negotiate and agree to. Each deal for you has to be a personal as well as a company commitment. Your role does not end when the signatures are recorded. In many respects it continues through the lifetime of the deal.

You must take a personal interest in what happens after the negotiation and be ready to use your good (and best) offices to get things put right that manifestly are wrong. Good and enduring personal relations between negotiators will lead to long-term relationships between their companies, and it is from this that the mutual prosperity of trading partners grows.

Your best action is always to follow through on a deal. Call the other guy on the phone or drop in to see him on your next visit, to check that everything that you agreed to is actually happening and that he is well satisfied with the outcome. In other words, you do not sign the contract, grab the cash, and run. Follow through and follow up if there are any problems. Your pride alone should incline you to do so, but your long-term best interests should make it mandatory.

Tenth, in deciding how to conduct your business affairs abroad, particularly when operating in parts of the world where social license is somewhat greater than it is elsewhere, you must be guided by what you feel comfortable doing rather than by what you feel is right or wrong.

This is by no means a prescription for abandoning the distinction between right and wrong—quite the reverse!—nor is it a prescription for turning you into a hardened cynic. The facts of life here are that many parts of the world with which the United States trades do have different standards of personal conduct and these standards influence whether you get business or even get around the country itself. You will have to learn to live with this and adapt to it, or you will not do business in those places.

Deciding on what is right in the circumstances is no easy

STYLES OF NEGOTIATING

EUROPEAN	AMERICAN	JAPANESE
State capitalist	Competitive capitalist	Welfare capitalist
Traditional individualism	Self-reliant individualism	Traditional collectivism
Status by background	Status by success	Status by position
Personal leadership	Personal leadership	Group consensus
Integrity oriented	Reward oriented	Respect oriented
Impatient	Very impatient	Patient
Fairly formal	Informal	Formal
Short preliminaries	Few preliminaries	Long preliminaries
Fair offers	Reasonable offers	Sky-high offers
Modest concessions	Few concessions	Large concessions
Item-by-item trade	Item-by-item trade	Linked package deal
Considerable authority	Total authority	No authority
Persuasive tactics	Aggressive tactics	Consensus tactics
Logical arguments	Arguments	Analysis of needs
Promises	Threats	Commitments
"Good deal"	"Best deal"	"Long-term deal"
Not losing	Winning	Succeeding

matter, and it is therefore a highly personal decision which you cannot pass on to somebody else. What you will be advised to do by people sitting on their safe and comfortable seats back home might be fine for an assembly of ostriches approaching a sandy beach but absolutely useless for you as you go down the ramp from your aircraft and approach the ranks of officialdom at customs and immigration (and the serried ranks of their colleagues along the corridors of the ministries you need to get past to complete your negotiations). It is you who will be faced with the moral dilemmas in Ogoland and you who must decide what to do about what you face there.

It would be presumptuous of me to advise you on such matters, except perhaps to suggest that you talk to the older hands about them on a country-by-country basis. Listen to what they have to say, reflect on the fact that billions of dollars worth of business is being conducted every year in the environment in question, and decide in each case what you feel most comfortable about doing (remember the sixth rule about your right to say no).

Negotiate abroad!

Your journey through this book is almost over. I hope that it is a prelude to many journeys that you will make in pursuit of your commercial interests. I began by asserting that negotiating principles are the same the world over but that the way the shots are played will vary from one culture to another. I have demonstrated some of the most salient differences between some of the world's cultures, though not exhaustively or comprehensively for every major country.

The book's central theme has been that it does not matter for what stakes you are negotiating; if you are negotiating abroad you will have to adapt your style to the dominant style of the people with whom you wish to do business, particularly if they have alternatives to what you are offering (which will almost certainly be the case in the competitive world markets we have today).

If you apply yourself to the task, approach every transaction with an open mind, spend as much time as you can going over the moves, the successes, and the setbacks you experience, and above all remember that you are the foreigner, then I have no doubt that you will be able to improve your international negotiating performance and join that small elite who successfully ply their wares anywhere that their companies send them.

Lastly, if you are passing through an airport, hotel, car rental office, ferry service, government corridor, company dining room, or whatever and you see me sitting around with not too much to do, why not amble across and introduce yourself. We can swap experiences over a cup or two of coffee or, if we are both in funds and on expense accounts, we might stretch ourselves and our budgets to a glass or two of the local nectar!

Index

Gavin Kennedy runs negotiating clinics and seminars in the United States, United Kingdom, Scandinavia, Australia, and South Africa, together with the coauthors of his first negotiating book, *Managing Negotiations*. He is also the author of *Everything Is Negotiable!* Gavin Kennedy is an economist teaching in the Business School at the University of Strathclyde. He is married, has five children, and lives in Edinburgh, Scotland.